WORKING WITH
PARENTS OF
BULLIES
AND
VICTIMS

For the children, families, and educators of the Red Lake Nation
and of the Rocori School District

WALTER B. ROBERTS, JR.

WORKING WITH PARENTS OF

BULLIES

AND

VICTIMS

CORWIN PRESS
A SAGE Publications Company
Thousand Oaks, CA 91320

For information:

Corwin Press
A Sage Publications Company
2455 Teller Road
Thousand Oaks, California 91320
www.corwinpress.com

Sage Publications India Pvt. Ltd.
B 1/I 1 Mohan Cooperative Industrial Area
Mathura Road, New Delhi 110 044
India

Sage Publications Ltd.
1 Oliver's Yard
55 City Road
London EC1Y 1SP
United Kingdom

Sage Publications Asia-Pacific Pte. Ltd.
33 Pekin Street #02-01
Far East Square
Singapore 048763

Printed in the United States of America

Library of Congress Cataloging-in-Publication Data

Roberts, Walter B.
Working with parents of bullies and victims / Walter B. Roberts, Jr.
    p. cm.
Includes bibliographical references and index.
ISBN 978-1-4129-5103-6 (cloth)
ISBN 978-1-4129-5104-3 (pbk.)
1. Bullying in schools—Prevention. 2. School management and organization—Parent participation. 3. School violence—Prevention. I. Title.

LB3013.3.R635 2008
371.7′82—dc22   2007017362

This book is printed on acid-free paper.

07   08   09   10   11   10   9   8   7   6   5   4   3   2   1

Acquisitions Editor:	Stacy Wagner
Managing Editor:	Jessica Allan
Editorial Assistant:	Joanna Coelho
Project Editor:	Astrid Virding
Copy Editor:	Gail Naron Chalew
Typesetter:	C&M Digitals (P) Ltd.
Proofreader:	Scott Oney
Indexer:	Juniee Oneida
Cover Designer:	Scott Van Atta

Contents

Preface

This is a companion volume to my book *Bullying From Both Sides: Strategic Interventions for Working With Bullies and Victims*, published in 2006 by Corwin Press. It is intended to further the excellent work of educators on the frontlines by expanding their skills in talking with parents about the thorny subject of bullying. It focuses on the educator-parent connection in working together as a team to help solve the problem on behalf of the child.

Often, educators find parents difficult to work with for any variety of reasons. Parents may have unreal expectations for what can and cannot be done for their child within the confines of our contemporary educational structures. They are often too tired to be able to adequately muster the type of home supervision necessary to assist their child in homework, discuss peer problems, or just simply keep up with the everyday Kid World pace, which seems to get faster and faster with each new technological invention. And let's be real, too: some parents are just difficult to engage in a meaningful effort to help their child. (How's that for reframing?)

On the flip side, parents often feel that educators care about their child only from a purely academic standpoint, that educators are more concerned about rules than the children who have to follow them, and that they never offer any *real* solutions to help solve whatever problem it is that the parents came to visit the teacher about in the first place.

Clearly, there is a miscommunication problem between parents and teachers. That miscommunication is often further magnified by cultural and socioeconomic barriers that can make the parties uneasy with one another because they simply do not understand enough about each other's lifestyles, dreams, and motivations to be able to truly trust one another in the mutual goal of helping the child.

One of the most difficult issues to discuss between the home and the school is peer-on-peer abuse. Whatever we choose to call it—bullying, taunting, teasing, intimidation, or hazing—the major stumbling block to sound educator-parent communication about this issue is the reality that, up until the last decade, both schools and parents have turned a blind eye to the problem. When there was a need for parent-educator collaboration to defeat the problem, both sides had few tools to offer each other except the worn-out "wisdom" of "maybe if they ignore it, it will go away."

One of the best strategies to solve bullying is the parent-educator connection.

This book is designed to provide a few more tools in the educator-parent toolbox for bridging the communication disconnect over the subject of bullying. Educators can no longer recommend that the solution to aggressive behaviors is discipline alone. Parents can no longer assume that they play no role or are helpless in working with their children to solve the bullying they receive. By increasing the adult supervision and guidance on *both* sides of the school fence—at home and on the school grounds—we will be better able to help our children during some of their darkest hours of need.

ACKNOWLEDGMENTS

No book is written in the absence of the advice and counsel of many. Please allow me to express my gratitude to a few of those who have guided me through the process of completing this one.

First and foremost, there are those from whom I have learned much, yet whom I cannot identify in order to protect their confidentiality. The stories from the children and adolescents who have suffered the misery of being physically intimidated and psychologically abused are deeply rooted in the heart of all of my efforts to end the scourge of bullying which plagues their lives. Likewise, the parents of those who have been targeted for such maltreatment have been gracious to share with me their frustrations and perceptions about how school personnel have both successfully and unsuccessfully responded to their requests for assistance. Their collective stories have helped formulate many of the techniques and strategies you will find in the book.

As always, my continued loyalty and belief in the power of each educator to change the life of a child is what encouraged me to tackle this largely unaddressed approach. While much is written about bullying, little has been offered to date for the largest group of adults who hold the promise of intervening in the bully-victim relationship—the educator. It is hoped that their application of the methods found within will expand their repertoire of personal and professional skills in defusing interpersonal conflict among their students.

Some specific individuals bear mentioning. Stacy Wagner, Corwin Press editor of my first book, *Bullying From Both Sides*, provided the dogged persistence and guidance to continue plugging away when the going became difficult. Stacy recognized that there was an entire extra book in the remnant of chapters not used in the first one. Her gentle way of offering me "suggestions" when I wanted to do something differently have only helped make this book better. Best of all, she tolerated my awful sense of humor. (Actually, I think she understood it.) Stacy has left Corwin Press to provide her expertise to another publishing company. I will miss her stewardship greatly and I know that Corwin Press feels the same.

However, because Stacy is such a pro at what she does, before she left she transitioned me to her assistant, Joanna Coelho. Joanna has many of the same gifts as Stacy, the greatest of which is the patience to put up with my wild ideas about what I think I know about book publishing. (Of course, I know nothing.) She has been able to take over the editorship of a book in the final stages of editing and production and make the segue seamless. I look forward to working with Joanna in the near future on the next book. (Now, if I can just get her to laugh at my jokes as much as Stacy did.)

Both Stacy and Joanna worked together to collect a group of reviewers for the drafts who provided invaluable observations, suggestions, and additional insights from their many various professional perspectives. Because of their willingness to give of their time in those reviews, many valuable tweaks and changes were made. I want to thank the following people:

JoLynn V. Carney, PhD
Associate Professor of Counselor
  Education
The Pennsylvania State University
University Park, PA

Leigh Cassidy
Professional High School Counselor
Eleanor Roosevelt High School
Greenbelt, MD

Laura M. Crothers
Assistant Professor
Duquesne University
Pittsburgh, PA

Steve Hutton
Consultant
Kentucky Center for Instructional
  Discipline
Villa Hills, KY

Toni Ippolito
School Counselor
Millburn High School
Millburn, NJ

Michael S. Kelly, PhD
Assistant Professor
Loyola University Chicago School of
  Social Work
Chicago, IL

Angil Littlejohn
Olweus Bullying Coordinator
Cabool Middle School
Cabool, MO

William Livers, MS, MSW
School Social Worker
Southwest Parke Community Schools
  District
Montezuma, IN

Rob Osborn
Anti-Bullying Strategy Manager
Leicestershire Children and Young
  People's Service and Anti-Bullying
  Alliance
Leicester, Leicestershire, England

Nancy A. Riestenberg
Violence Prevention Specialist
Minnesota Department of Education
Roseville, MN

Sandi Stein, MSW, LGSW
School Social Worker
Edina Public Schools
Edina, MN

As always, my family continues to be supportive and tolerant of my many gadfly endeavors, be they writing, workshops, consultations, or legislative in nature. They are the foundation under which I grow, and the roots grow deeper with each passing year.

And, as corny as it may seem (but for those who know me, they will understand), I want to give special recognition to Ranger the Mighty Wonder Dog, who has been by my side every waking minute that I have spent working on this book. While his motives may have been less than noble ("I'm just here for the possibility that you'll drop the sandwich."), he has put up with the highs and lows of editing and the loss of materials due to a dying (or demon possessed!) hard drive, and he has heard every mumbled word that I speak to myself as I think out loud during the creative process. Through it all, regardless of my mood du jour, he has offered the most valuable gift the world has to offer—unconditional positive regard.

Thanks, good friend. Now that this ordeal is over, let's go fishing!

About the Author

Walter Roberts, Jr. is a Professor of Counselor Education at Minnesota State University, Mankato. He began his career in education as a classroom teacher in 1978 and later served as a school counselor before moving to higher education in 1993. In addition to being licensed for private practice, he has extensive public policy experience in mental health and school safety issues, consults and testifies with legislators and the judicial system, and is a frequent source for the media on counseling-related issues. *Bullying From Both Sides*, his first book published by Corwin Press in 2006, continues to be a best-seller. Requests for information regarding workshops, keynotes, and consultations can be directed to walter.roberts@mnsu.edu. Due to the large volume of mail he receives, please specify "Bully Inquiry" in the subject header of any e-mail inquiry.

CHAPTER ONE

Every Parent's Nightmare— and *Yours*, Too!

It is one of every parent's nightmares: what to do when a child faces a problem that the parents do not think they know how to help solve. One dilemma that figures in many parents' nightmares is their feelings of helplessness when a child reports to them that he or she is being bullied. Parents cannot accompany their children 24 hours a day to guide and protect them through all the travails of life. Even if they could, to do so would be debilitating in the long run. Children must learn to interact with their peers successfully, and they must learn how to interact with those peers whom they find difficult. However, children also need adult assistance during those times when they do not feel as if they have the resources to solve their own problems with peers who are difficult.

Parents often grow frustrated when they turn to educators for advice and counsel about what to do in instances when a child is bullied. One simple recommendation, which has been offered for many years, is to give back in kind what one is receiving. This may well be the advice that was passed down from the parents' own mothers and fathers, which, of course, was the solution from *their* mothers and fathers and so on down the genealogical tree. We know, of course, that this simplest of recommendations is not always the one that works best. Returning in kind the same treatment that one receives may solve a problem for the immediate moment, but it will likely only create additional long-term problems as soon as the bullies regroup. Bullies are creative in their abilities to up the ante when challenged. They are not likely to let a victim have the last word in an interaction, particularly in a public confrontation in which the bully or the bully's companions lost the challenge. The only thing worse for victims than being confronted by bullies is encountering a mob that has been embarrassed by the target of its aggravations.

Parents and educators must remember the Number One Cardinal Rule of Being a Kid: *I will come to adults only for advice in the most dire of circumstances.* This rule, of course, becomes more stringent as children become adolescents, when the definition of "dire circumstances" equates with things like plagues, fires, and frogs raining down from the heavens. So, if this is the playing field in which children navigate, educators must create their own Number One Cardinal Rule of Being an Educator: *If a child comes to me with something viewed as a problem, then I need to pay attention because it must really, really be a problem because I know about the Number One Cardinal Rule of Being a Kid!* And while we're making up all sorts of cardinal rules, let's make a corollary to the last one. We'll call it the Number One Cardinal Rule of Educators in Dealing With Parents Concerned About Bullying: *I promise that I will try to do what is within my power to work with the parent on this problem, no matter how many buttons of mine this parent pushes.*

WHO WILL BENEFIT FROM THIS BOOK?

This book is written for educators to help them accomplish two goals. First, it is intended to provide workable ideas to help educators of all stripes—be they classroom teachers, administrators, school counselors, paraprofessionals, or even day care providers—communicate with parents about the difficult topic of bullying. Second, it is designed to give educators tips to help parents work with their children at home in dealing with the problem. I sometimes use "we" and "us" in this book. That is because I too am still an educator. My personal educational journey over the last 30 years has led me from the K–12 classroom, to the school counselor's office, into private practice as a licensed professional counselor, and now into higher education as a professor—but my heart and soul is still that of the practitioner. I believe that, too often, those of us in higher education lose sight of what is most important about our work: the practicality and usefulness of the knowledge we impart to those who will ultimately be applying it. I hope you will find the information here helpful in making life better for all concerned—you as educator, the parent who is concerned about a child, the child, and, ultimately, society as a whole.

Bullying is not just a problem for those who receive it on the ends of their noses or in a screeching defamatory Web site posted for all the world to see. Bullying is an educator's problem too. It diminishes a child's ability to learn, and, in this day of testing anything that moves, some will ultimately draw the conclusion that the child's low standardized scores are the teacher's fault. For both the teacher and the administrator, bullying can lead to accusations of negligence that, with a savvy lawyer, can end up in court (Dawson, 2006; National School Boards Association, 2005; Rispoli, 2006; Schultz, 2004). For the parents, it can cause tremendous anxiety about their children's health and safety when they drop them off on the school grounds each morning. It can even lead to marital discord when one parent believes that ignoring the problem is the best thing to do and the other believes that doing "something" (usually contacting the school) is the proper way to proceed.

Bullying, as well as other forms of intimidation that our children experience, is *everyone's* problem. Although bullying will never be prevented or stopped in all instances, its incidence can certainly be reduced by increased adult supervision combined with the implementation of curricular strategies that enable children to find solutions to their own dilemmas when adults are not around. In the end, the ultimate goal of education must be giving children the tools and information necessary to make sound decisions on their own.

THE HIGH COST OF IGNORING THE PROBLEM

Educators must accept their roles as critical players in the bullying solution process. For far too long adults in supervisory positions have made excuses for *not* getting involved in the bully-victim dyad. It is an inarguable fact: attempts to address the issue have been feeble at best. It was only when our kids started killing themselves and others—literally—as an outcry from the bullying that they had been receiving for years that we begrudgingly agreed that well, yes, maybe intimidation in schools *is* a problem after all.

Yet, a decade following the school shootings at Columbine, with the 2007 event at Virginia Tech in which another young adult in an educational setting who felt victimized lashed out violently against his tormentors, we see that the problem still exists. Consider some recent examples of the effects of bullying that our children continue to tolerate :

- 2005, Tonganoxie, Kansas: A federal jury awarded $205,000 to a male student who had been sexually harassed at school for years. School personnel were held responsible for failing to intervene on the student's behalf in spite of widespread knowledge within the school that the maltreatment was ongoing.[1]

- 2005, Colorado Springs: Three high school females were suspended after posting a defamatory Web site about two other females. More than 70 students had access to the off-school Web site. One of the posts included the comment, "If they can break my best friend's heart then I can just as easily break their necks."[2]

- 2006, Suwannee Country, Florida: A frustrated and angry grandfather of one of two second-grade girls who had been tied to the playground monkey bars with their shoelaces by three older second-grade boys called the school and threatened to come with his shotgun and straighten things out his own way. The threat put the entire school district in security lockdown mode.[3]

- 2006, Warroad, Minnesota: Internet chatter among students intimidated by bullying escalated into threats of shootings at school. Administrators canceled classes for protection until the threats could be investigated and then suspended six students pending the filing of charges as the investigation continued.[4]

- 2006, New York City: A bus driver was charged with encouraging 11- and 12-year-old students to bully other students on his bus in order to comply with his self-designed 12-tier ranking system. The ranking system was to be enforced with the admonition, "Mercy will not be tolerated."[5]

- 2006, Green Bay, Wisconsin: Three high school students, aged 17 and 18, were arrested before they could launch a Columbine-style massacre at their school. They had planned the attack for years, stemming from their frustration at being bullied and harassed, one because of his weight and special education status.[6]

- 2006, Cazenovia, Wisconsin: A 15-year-old student in a rural school shot and killed the principal, who had recently suspended him for illegal tobacco use. The student claimed that he was also angry about being called "fag" and "faggot" by his peers and felt as if no one was listening to him.[7]

- 2006, North Pole, Alaska: Six seventh graders plotted to kill classmates on their hit-list of classmates who had been bullying them. The plan was developed over a series of months and was to take place in school.[8]

- 2006, Riverton, Kansas: Five high school males were arrested within hours of beginning a school assault on the seventh anniversary of the Columbine massacre. At least one of the five had revealed the plans during a Myspace.com chat. Those targeted included individuals who had bullied the conspirators and called them names.[9]

- 2006, Joplin, Missouri: A seventh-grade student fired an assault rifle into the ceiling of his middle school after being confronted by the school principal. His mother reported that he frequently came home from school with injuries inflicted by other students. "He would come home crying, begging us not to send him back to school," she said.[10]

Clearly, we have much work to do.

HOW EDUCATORS HAVE OVERLOOKED PARENTS AS PARTNERS

To a large extent, the success of the work we all must do to protect our children and prevent bullying depends on bringing in an overlooked and neglected piece of the solutions equation—parents. Unfortunately, parents, for the most part, are often not well versed in how to be a part of that equation. Truth be told, educators are frequently reluctant to include parents in most of the educational domain. Educators sometimes feel that parents are a part of the problem, whatever the problem *de jour* is. Parents may be viewed as overreactive, overemotional, and biased. Parents sometimes seem to wear blinders, lacking peripheral vision when it comes to their child. They are seen as whiners, complainers, and, in the end, as just not knowing what is best for their own child. We educators always know what is best. After all, *we* are the educators, right?

Parents, in turn, may have their own misperceptions about educators. Often those complaints revolve around our own type of restricted vision. We are sometimes viewed as arrogant and as not listening—to both them and their child. We are seen as focusing only on the child as a test score and not as the total little emerging human being that he or she is. Some parents, remember, are "invited" to come to school only when there is a problem with their child.

There is probably a little bit of truth in both sides of the equation.

Is there any wonder that parents and educators have a history of poor collaboration? Such uneasiness, if not outright defensiveness, by both parties often dooms conferences and needed collaborations from the get-go.

We all—parents and educators—simply have to get over and beyond all of this mistrust if we are going to work toward mutual solutions on behalf of the children we claim to care so much about. That means we have to have mutual respect, we must acknowledge that we each hold different parts of the puzzle, and we must be willing to work around our differences and our biases for the sake of our kids. When it comes to solving the problems of bullying, Smith and Myron-Wilson (1998) said it best: "Parents need to be brought in as part of the solution" (p. 414).

To that end, let's start by dispelling some of the *misinformation* that characterizes educators' views about parents' perceptions of educators. That's right, many of the things that we *think* that parents believe about us are simply *not* true!

Analyses of data from 2002–2003 by the U.S. Department of Education's National Center for Education Statistics (NCES; 2005, 2006) contradict many of the myths held by educators concerning parental attitudes about school personnel.

- In 2003, 58% of parents of children in Grades 3 through 12 were "very satisfied" with their child's school and academic standards, 59% felt the same about their child's teachers, and 60% gave the highest marks for the order and discipline in the school (NCES, 2006, Indicator 38, "School Characteristics and Climate"). These percentages were equal to or higher than the same indicators for the years 1993 and 1999. In fact, 71.4% of parents with children in the third to fifth grades in 2003 rated themselves as "very satisfied" with their child's teachers!

Do those statistics reflect the image of parents spending all their time at home conjuring up spells and sticking pins in a voodoo doll with the label "My Child's Teacher" on it? Hardly. Yet, although these data do not indicate that the "vast majority" of parents think that educators are doing a "horrible" job teaching their children, they do imply that 40% of parents are floating around out there who do not rate us as splendid. That does not mean, however, that the only other options available after "very satisfied" were "wretched," "miserable," and "hopeless." Quite to the contrary, those other categories were "somewhat satisfied," "somewhat dissatisfied," or "very dissatisfied" (NCES, 2006, Indicator 38, "School Characteristics and Climate"). And how many of those parents fell into those aforementioned pin-sticking-voodoo-doll categories? Contrary to our opinions, not very many.

- In 2003, 32.5% of parents rated themselves as "somewhat satisfied" overall with their child's school, 6.7% were "somewhat dissatisfied," and 3.2% were "very dissatisfied" (NCES, 2006, Table 38–1, "Percentage of Children in Grades 3–12 With Parents Who Were Very Satisfied With Various Aspects of the School Their Child Attends, by Selected Characteristics: 1993, 1999, 2003").

Doing the math on those last two categories comes up with a whopping 10%—that's right, *10%!* Let that figure soak in a minute. Contrary to all the talking heads who like to bash education—and our *own* assumptions about what we *think* that parents think about us—only 10% of parents indicated that they were dissatisfied with their children's schools. The misperception that leads us to be skittish in our interactions with parents because we *think* that they don't like us often supports *our assumption* that parents are difficult to work with, when quite the opposite is likely to be true!

HOW TO USE THIS BOOK WITH PARENTS

Educators play an important role in bridging this miscommunication gap, and that is exactly what this book is designed to help educators do. In addition to giving background information, each chapter has lists of talking points and approaches that educators can suggest to parents when they approach the school for help.

The ideas in this book will negate parental perceptions that (1) school personnel have nothing to offer in the fight to reduce intimidation in educational settings and (2) that they—the parents—are totally dependent on school personnel for solutions. Educators and supervisory personnel might well want to create a handout of the suggestions found in this book to give to parents (all I ask is that you cite the source!). Additionally, this book is written so that educators can help parents understand how school systems work in solving bullying problems in educational settings. The book is written for both educators and parents to level the playing field of understanding and increase the chances of better communication in the parent-educator collaboration toward violence prevention.

What we want to create is an **educator-parent partnership** in solving the problem of bullying within our schools. Such an alliance is based on the belief that *both* the parent and the educator possess solutions to the problems that *both* groups are concerned about solving. It means that *both* parties understand that by working *together* they increase the chances of finding the solutions necessary to improve student behaviors and help children learn. In the end, it is important to remember that children need us to act like adults in order to help them learn by example the lessons about problem solving. They must learn that the best problem solving emerges when people put aside any differences they may have for the common good.

So, let's get started! First, it will be important to review some of the basic dynamics of intimidation and cite several examples that will remind us of the repercussions that bullying has for its victims and our society.

NOTES

1. Cronkleton, R. (2005, August 12). Taunted teen wins federal suit. *Kansas City* [Missouri] *Star.* Retrieved August 13, 2005, from http://www.kansascity.com

2. Newsome, B. (2005, November 19). Students suspended over website. *Gazette* [Colorado Springs, Colorado]. Retrieved November 19, 2005, from http://www.gazette .com

3. Fultz, V. (2006, February 9). Schools locked down after scare: Officials issue code red alert for entire school system. *Suwanee* [Suwanee County, Florida] *Democrat*. Retrieved December 9, 2006, from http://www.suwanneedemocrat.com

4. Associated Press. (2006, February 6). "Credible threat" closes Warroad schools. WCCO-TV [Minneapolis, Minnesota]. Retrieved December 9, 2006, from http://wcco.com

5. Seaberg, M., & Sclafani, T. (2006, February 3). Meet Jaba the nut: Driver hit for "Star Wars"fight club on school bus. *New York Daily News.* Retrieved December 9, 2006, from http://nydailynews.com

6. Imrite, R. (2006, September 17). Accused teen's mom says he was bullied at school. *Press Gazette* [Green Bay, Wisconsin]. Retrieved December 11, 2006, from http:// www.greenbaypressgazette.com

7. Sander, L. (2006, September 30). Wisconsin principal is shot, killed in struggle with teen. [Minneapolis, Minnesota] *Star Tribune*, p. A4.

8. Johnson, K. (2006, April 23). Students had hit list, mayor says. *USA Today.* Retrieved April 24, 2006, from http://www.usatoday.com

9. Kabel, M. (2006, April 21). School death plot revealed. *Kansas City* [Missouri] *Star.* Retrieved April 24, 2006, from http://www.kansascity.com

10. Pippin, M. (2006, November 17). Middle school bullies and their victims. *Joplin* [Missouri] *Daily.* Retrieved December 9, 2006, from http://joplindaily.com

CHAPTER TWO

What Bullying and Teasing Do to Everyone—Kids, Adults, and Communities

"Sticks and stones may break my bones, but words will never hurt me."

This children's taunt was first listed in Folk Phrases of Four Counties *(1894) by G. F. Northall and is first attested in the United States in* Miss Lindsey *(1936) by S. G. Gibbons. The* Morris Dictionary of Word and Phrase Origins *(Morris & Morris, 1977/1988) also notes that the first use of this phrase is found in* Folk Phrases. *According to the* Random House Dictionary of Popular Proverbs and Sayings *(Titelman, 1996), this proverb is found in varying forms: "Sticks and stones may break my bones, but hard words cannot hurt me"; "Sticks and stones can break my bones, but words can never hurt me"; and "Sticks and stones will break my bones, but lies will never hurt me."*

From Phrase Finder Discussion Forum (2000)

I n *Bullying From Both Sides,* I give a more detailed review of all of the definitions and nuances of bullying. The reader will find it helpful to refer to Chapter 2 in that book (see pp. 13–20) to obtain a deeper understanding of the problem and its full context. For the sake of avoiding duplication, we do not repeat all of that information here. However, it is useful to review here some of the basic ground rules and definitions so you are better able to explain and summarize the problem to those parents whom we want working with us in our newly created partnership mode.

Bullying and **teasing** are often considered to be the same. Dan Olweus, of Norway, known as the "grandfather" of bullying prevention programs used in many European and North American schools, created the generally accepted definition of the behavior. Olweus (1993) conceptualizes bullying as the exposure to long-term, repeated negative actions on the part of one or more persons. It can be designed to intimidate psychologically, physically, or both. *Bullying* tends to be more physical than teasing or taunting and is stereotypically associated with boys. *Teasing* is generally conceptualized as being more verbal and is assumed to be more likely to occur with girls and at younger ages within both sexes. However, both behaviors are more complex than their stereotypes. Each is clearly designed to obtain some form of gain for the one who is intimidating the other. The **aggressor** of the bullying activity—let's call it what it is—may be looking to gain status among peers or something more tangible, such as items stolen from victims. There is never anything fair in the bully-victim relationship: The bully always has the upper hand, whether by strength, by numbers, or psychologically.

Bullying occurs along a **continuum** that ranges from mild to severe. Minor and sporadic instances of harassment, such as name calling, gossiping, or pushing and shoving, are examples of **mild** intimidation. When these behaviors become more frequent and harsh, they are worthy of classification as **moderate** bullying. Instances of bullying that are considered **severe** include physical assault, outrageous and clearly defamatory rumors, or ganging together to engage in aggressive activities against targets (see Figure 2.1, p. 16, in *Bullying From Both Sides* for more details). The use of electronic communication (e.g., text messages, cell phones, Web pages) to intimidate others, or **cyberbullying**, is another method by which individuals can be bullied.

Most children during their formative years have experienced some sort of bullying behavior. They may very well have engaged in it as well. The *Journal of the American Medical Association* reported that nearly 30% of children in Grades 6 through 10 had some kind of involvement in the bully-victim dyad, in either role (Nansel et al., 2001). Although the vast majority are able to navigate this tortuous physical and psychological obstacle course, others do not do it so successfully. What follows are two examples of the long-term damage that bullying can have on the human soul.

DEATH COMES TO LAKE WOBEGON

When I was working on drafts for *Bullying From Both Sides*, a 15-year-old ninth-grade student in a rural Minnesota school district shot and killed two other students inside the high school building (Meryhew, Burcum, & Schmickle, 2003). Eighteen months after that, another Minnesota child killed nine others—four adults, five classmates, and then himself—and wounded five other students in a rampage in his tribal school at the Red Lake Nation of the Chippewa (Meryhew, Haga, Padilla, & Oakes, 2005). Prior to the massacre at Virginia Tech in 2007, it was the largest loss of life in a school shooting since Columbine in 1999. Death, it seems, had come to the children and families in the state of the mythical Lake Wobegon, that place where all the children are above average.

In the first case, which occurred at Rocori High School, court documents verified every news report from eyewitnesses that the young man was motivated to seek revenge for the taunting he had received from another 14-year-old classmate. However, his initial effort at vengeance went awry. The first shot from his handgun struck a senior who was in a gym area, who died almost immediately. There was no connection between the shooter and the senior—he was simply an unintended victim.

Adolescent victims of harassment who intend to strike back at their tormentors and whose efforts backfire are often shocked into recognizing the realities of what they are doing and stop their attack, especially when they see an unintended victim of their action suffer an abuse similar to that which they have had to experience. The jolt of the act itself is often enough to stop the avenger from continuing. Such was not the case in Rocori. In the chaos that followed, the shooter continued his pursuit of the original target. He chased him to another area of the school and fired another round point-blank that would inevitably prove fatal, two weeks later. What might have happened or what the intent of the victim-attacker was after shooting the second student is unclear. Fortunately, a well-respected teacher heroically confronted the shooter and commanded him to drop his handgun. The student complied. He was found guilty and must serve a minimum of 30 years in prison before he will be eligible for parole.

Minnesotans rightfully mourned the tragedy in that school district. When school shootings dominated the news in the late 1990s, Minnesota had fortunately dodged such catastrophes. In fact, up until Rocori, the Midwest had been largely left untouched by the school shootings that had occurred across the country. But that tragedy was just a precursor to what was yet to come.

In March 2005, a deeply troubled 16-year-old high school junior embarked on a shooting spree that began at his home and eventually spread to Red Lake High School. Although many factors contributed to his personal distress, one of the issues that he spoke about before the incident was his sense of isolation from peers. He felt intimidated by his classmates for his style of dress and self-proclaimed Gothic lifestyle. Much of his distress was posted in Internet chat rooms. He even created sophisticated computer animations detailing a virtual synopsis of what he ended up doing. His pain and plans were not unknown. Later investigation revealed that 39 peers knew something about the shooter's mind-set and potential plans before he carried them out (Ragsdale, 2006). However, only one of those who possessed this information was tried and sentenced to serve jail time. He was sentenced to one year at a private treatment facility and, on release, will be on probation until the age of 21.

Because the shooter committed suicide at the scene, there are many questions left unanswered for the people of the Red Lake Nation. However, the shooter did not hide the personal anguish in his life. Here are his words verbatim (with references to others deleted), as posted on one of several Internet chat rooms in which he participated. (Sources for these postings have been moved from their original sites for privacy and legal reasons. Interested parties may contact the author directly for assistance in tracking down the archived sites.)

May 13, 2004 23:06

They pegged me as a possible school shooter earlier this year, or wait, that was last month.

Apparently someone was supposed to shoot up the school on 4/20, and there was alot of buzz around me, and for good reasons I guess.

I wear combat boots (with my pant legs tucked into them), wear a trench coat, and at the last basketball game my friend . . . (who happens to wear a black trench coat like mine), did a "Sieg Heil" during the national anthem (for shock value), so they had us pegged as "Trench Coat Mafia." My "friend" . . . even said that I fit the profile of a school shooter that she saw on 60 minutes . . .

I happen to be "not so popular," Gothic (in the sense that I wear nothing but black, spike my hair in "devil" horns, and listen to music like Cradle of Filth and KoRn), and happen to be an emotionally disturbed person, if you could call me that. So it's really no problem slapping a label on someone because they fit the stereotype. And no, I wasn't the one who did the threat. On "Game day" (4/20) the Feds were all around the place, watching, cop cars on nearly every corner around the school and a few large unmarked black vans sitting around, I bet they were on standby. So they WERE prepared for something to happen.

Nov. 8, 2004 13:30

[In response to an apology from another chat room subscriber who had downplayed the level of mental pain that the shooter had previously expressed.]

Would you please try to be a little bit more considerate?

I had went through alot of things in my life that had driven me to a darker path than most choose to take. I split the flesh on my wrist with a box opener, painting the floor of my bedroom with blood I shouldn't have spilt. After sitting there for what seemed like hours (which apparently was only minutes), I had the revelation that this was not the path.

It was my decision to seek medical treatment, as on the other hand I could've chose to sit there until enough blood drained from my downward lascerations on my wrists to die.

I am now on Anti-depressants, and just because you've probably never been through anything Like I have doesn't give you the write to say what you have.

I am trying to turn my life around, I'm trying really hard, the attitudes of people like you are what set me back.

On his MSN Web site in the "My Picture" section, he posted a frame from the fictional Columbine movie, *Elephant*, which showed the two protagonists with duffle bags entering the school where they would later commit their massacre. In the "A Little About Me" section, he wrote the following: *16 years of accumulated rage suppressed by nothing more than brief glimpses of hope, which have all faded to black. I can feel the urges within slipping through the cracks, the leash I can no longer hold.* His "Favorite Things" were as follows: *[Moments] where control becomes completely unattainable . . . times when maddened psycho paths briefly open the gates to hell, and let chaos flood through . . . those individuals who care enough to reclaim their place . . .*

Clearly, here was a young man in deep pain. The intervention of *just one* caring adult whom he respected might well have changed the course of history.

Shortly after the Red Lake massacre, the Chippewa Nation held a ceremony on the steps of the state capitol building in St. Paul to mourn the loss of life at Red Lake. I was there, along with 500 others, mostly members of the Native American nations of Minnesota. A bitter wind marred an otherwise cloudless sky. The mood on the ground was as sobering as the wind. The faces of the elders reflected the deep grief felt by everyone in attendance. Tribal nation speakers called for an end to violence across the spectrum of humanity. Drumming and singing honored the deceased, and a traditional Native American smudging ceremony was held to cleanse all of the participants of negative influences. Everyone shed tears, their emotions still raw from the questions about how such a terrible incident could have occurred and what messages young people must have about life in general to act in such a fashion.

These two tragedies have forever changed the communities in which they occurred, yet they serve as a reminder that, for many children, nothing has changed. There is still peer-on-peer abuse that demands prevention and intervention, and there are still children who feel as if they have nowhere else to turn when experiencing their most deep-seated pains.

We cannot stop all of the pain in our children's lives, but we can reduce some specific types. Curbing intimidation within educational settings is certainly within educators' capacities.

WHEN INTERVENTION STOPS TRAGEDY

What finally came to the mythical Lake Wobegon in 2003 and 2005 could just as readily have happened years before—and almost did. One of my dear friends who is a school counselor in another part of the state and his principal prevented a school shooting in 2002.

Word came that a student in the school who was being intimidated by a group of students was afraid of being attacked during the lunch hour and that he might very well have brought a gun with him that day for protection. This information came to the school counselor's attention about five minutes before the bell was to ring for the lunch period. The school counselor notified his principal, who called the police, and together they then took immediate action. First, they determined the student's whereabouts by looking at his class schedule. Second, they made a quick search of his locker to ascertain whether or not the weapon was there. It was not. Third, they moved to the classroom where the student was scheduled to be and opened the door slowly.

The plan was to calmly surround the student and escort him from the classroom. As fate would have it, the class was watching a video—with a substitute teacher, no less—and the room was pitch dark except for the streak of light that came through the open door. But as another stroke of fate would have it, that streak of light happened to fall across the row of seats where the student sat. My friend and his principal entered the room as if it was nothing out of the ordinary, just a stop-by visit; in fact, my friend even cracked a joke to the substitute about the quality of the video in progress while walking across the back of the room. The two of them then walked up to the student of concern, each gently taking one of his arms to control its movement, and walked him outside into the hallway.

Five seconds later, they found a pistol with a full clip in the student's sweatshirt. He had attended all of his classes that day with the gun. The information provided to the school counselor had, indeed, been credible, and in this instance, because there had been an accurate warning, school personnel were able to respond effectively.

THE PAIN THAT RESONATES TO THE BONE

Whatever the case and whichever examples I might have chosen to use here, nothing that I could ever write could convey more accurately the voices of affected children and adolescents than their own words. Theirs are the voices of deep hurt and anguish, the kind of agony that afflicts the heart and soul and is not forgotten easily, if ever. It is a pain that resonates to the bone.

Although high-profile incidents of school violence linked to bullying grab our attention when they occur—at least until the press goes away—the truth is that *right now* as you read these words there are young people, *perhaps several in your own school and whom you know,* who find themselves in such desperate situations that they contemplate irrational acts to end their torment—either by turning inward through self-harm or by exploding outward through a revenge fantasy in which they settle their pain through violence. **Bullycide** is the term that we use today to label acts of suicide when those who feel that they have no other solution to their torment except via "escaping" personal pain kill themselves. The frightening thing is that we are seeing an increase in such behaviors among middle-school-aged children—both boys and girls. We also know that, ironically, it is often the victims of bullying who end up hurting others as they bring weapons to schools to protect themselves from their tormentors (Carney & Merrell, 2001).

HOW EVERYONE LOSES WHEN BULLYING OCCURS

Hasn't this been a cheery chapter? It's enough to depress us all and make us want somebody else to deal with the problem. And that's just the point. Too often in the face of all the incredibly difficult issues that we educators face in the school setting, we pick and choose our battles, prioritizing those things that "must" be done and sacrificing or postponing the "less important" ones for later—and then, because the workload in our schools is so overwhelming, we just never seem to get back to those less important items until they pop back up on our radar screens as a must. Those of us in education understand the need to prioritize our job demands and that the tsunami of work never decreases—the waves only get bigger year after year.

But here's the sad truth about our taking that approach to the issue of bully-ing and intimidation among the children and adolescents in our schools—it's a problem for *us* as well as our students, whether we think so or not. How, you ask? Go back and reread some of those terrible incidents we covered in these first two chapters. Mercifully, the chances that a high-profile incident of school violence will erupt in our schools now are *lower* than a decade ago. The school safety and juvenile justice data all confirm this downward trend (see the National Center for Education Statistics at http://nces.ed.gov and the Bureau of Justice Statistics of the U.S. Department of Justice at http://www.ojp.usdoj.gov for the latest updates). What is more likely to happen, as we have previously seen, is that if a violent act in the school does occur, it will involve the use of more dangerous weapons and spread to more parties than just one particular individual (Newman, Fox, Harding, Mehta, & Roth, 2004). Innocent bystanders are often hurt in addition to the original target.

When victims strike back at their tormentors and when bullying goes unabated, the *whole school loses*. The overall school climate is affected negatively in the follow-ing ways:

- Students feel unsafe when they know that bullying occurs to others because they know that it can also happen to them.

- Students who feel unsafe in school do less well academically because they are distracted by the fear of intimidation from others or by making plans on how to avoid such intimidation.

- Parents lose faith in the school in which bullying is tolerated. They believe that educators cannot be trusted to safeguard their children.

- Educators within the school often bicker among themselves when some faculty address the problem and others do not. This is especially true when a perception exists that administrators ignore or deny that a problem exists while the faculty is willing to address the problem.

If this list is not enough, let's add one more item to consider, which—sadly, for all the wrong reasons—ends up being the one to which reluctant schools end up responding: faculty, school administrators, and school boards all face the potential of legal action for not preventing "foreseeable" incidences of intimidation.

When all else fails to motivate school personnel to take action, the legal beagles will be more than glad to do so. Parents have had enough of what is considered these days to be behavior that is *preventable*, and they are less afraid to push the legal option than ever before (Limber & Snyder, 2006). Why? Because education has been *reactive* and not *proactive* in addressing the problem, and that is *inexcusable* given what we know about bullying today. Parents are tired of being given the explanation, "We didn't know that it was happening," when it comes to bullying behaviors directed toward their children, whether that explanation is true or not.

It doesn't have to be that way, and that is why you have chosen to read this book. Educators *can* intervene effectively to break the cycle of bullying and prevent many of the tragedies that we have read about in these first two chapters from happening again. To be most effective, however, we need a **team approach** that enlists the assistance of parents in doing all that adults can humanly do to decrease bullying in Kid World. Now let's move forward and learn about some of the reasons why parents find it difficult to work with school personnel.

CHAPTER THREE

Why Parents Complain About Schools' Responses to Bullying

This is a difficult chapter to write because I respect educators so much and have had the opportunity to work with so many excellent ones throughout my lifetime. Their role modeling is what has helped make me who I am today, and I am very grateful for that.

> *They just didn't do anything. I called and talked to them until I was blue in the face and nothing changed. Finally, we just pulled her out and homeschooled her. At least we knew she was safe here.*
>
> Mother of a third-grade girl

But there is another side to education that I am embarrassed to have to admit exists. It's that side in which educators fail to respond to bullying either because, through a lack of support, knowledge, or techniques, they do not have the resources at their disposal to know how to respond to bullying when it occurs in schools, or, worse, because they think that child and adolescent peer-to-peer intimidation is acceptable and nothing to bother about. All of the quotes in this chapter are real. They come from professional consultations that I have done with parents, schools, and communities. The names, locations, and circumstances have obviously been changed to provide for both privacy and confidentiality.

There is absolutely no excuse for ignoring intimidation among children in our schools, whether public, private, or parochial! Why does this behavior occur among adults in supervisory positions? *Because we let it happen!* Although educators are not responsible for peer intimidation in the school setting, many times—not every time, but far more times than it should happen—we allow attitudes and behaviors that, tacitly or explicitly, enable such abuses to occur. That is just a plain, hard, cold fact. Most of the time it happens as a result of those busy workloads discussed

17

in earlier chapters that force us to pick our battles and let the "small stuff" go. But we have learned the hard way that when it comes to bullying, it's not so "small" in Kid World.

The fallout from this failure to respond effectively to the problem of intimidation in schools has hurt educator credibility. In spite of the glowing "very satisfied" majority of parents out there, there are other sets of statistics floating around that concern all of us.

PARENTS' ATTITUDES TOWARD PUBLIC SCHOOLS: THE STATISTICS

Although the most recent Phi Delta Kappa/Gallup (PDK/G) Poll of the Public's Attitudes Toward the Public Schools (Rose & Gallup, 2006) verifies many of the same positive opinions about the public school system as found by the NCES (2005, 2006) reports mentioned in Chapter 1, it also reports some cracks in that façade. Here are two such perceptions today that are specifically related to bullying:

- The biggest problems affecting local public schools include the lack of control and discipline (11%) and fighting (5%).[1]

- Lack of support from parents (96%) and administrators (93%) and poor working conditions within schools (92%) are the major reasons why teachers leave the classroom, many within the first few years of teaching.[2]

Although 11% and 5% may appear to be small percentages, the people who hold these opinions, whom we might want to categorize as overly reactive, nonetheless help spread perceptions within the community that all is not well within our local schools.

And whether true or not, the rumor mill continues to grind when such perceptions exist among parents—like the mother of the third-grade girl noted above who thought that the schools "just don't do anything" about intimidation when it occurs. More often than not, such perceptions are incorrect, but parents who feel slighted may persist in their claims that you "didn't do anything" because they did not have full access to all of the details of exactly what you *did* do or of the number of times before this incident that you *prevented* something from occurring. Sometimes, *we* are not even aware of the times we prevented or interrupted mischief in the making because those actions are part of our regular, everyday vigilance. It is difficult to share with parents how good we really are when we don't even know it ourselves.

Then, of course, there is the thorny little problem of the math. In a community of 50,000, that 11% figure in the PDK/G Poll who believe that schools have trouble with the control and discipline of their students translates into 5,500 potential gossip mongers spreading additional venom about how the "schools don't do anything," how they "don't control those kids up there," and, sakes alive, those kids are just "running naked up and down the hallways!"

Well, maybe the rumors are not *that* bad, but you know how things get out of hand. Still, when it comes to our responses to bullying, the perception that we "don't do anything" is out there, which then can lend itself to that 96% of the PDK/G Poll public who believe that we don't receive enough parental support in trying to do our jobs, thus encouraging new teachers to leave. So is the tail wagging the dog here? Do parents who buy into the belief that the schools have no control and discipline (the 11%) eagerly share that opinion with anyone who will listen and thus end up dissuading virtually everyone in the general public (hey, 96% *is* almost everybody!) from being more supportive of our efforts to provide just that?

The latest information available from the NCES about student reports of bullying poses another pesky problem for us (DeVoe & Kaffenberger, 2005). The NCES analysis of data from the 2001 National Crime Victimization Survey (NCVS) reports the following:

- 14% of students aged 12 through 18 report being bullied directly, indirectly, or both.[3]

- A startling 24% of sixth graders reported being bullied in some fashion.[4]

- Bullying was no less likely to occur at a public school than a private one.[5]

- Students who were bullied in some fashion were more likely to also have been criminally victimized through acts of serious violence and property theft.[6]

- Victims of bullying were more likely to carry some type of weapon to school for protection.[7]

- Bullied students experience more academic failure than nonbullied peers.[8]

Do we think that tales of these student experiences don't make it home to moms and dads? We're fooling ourselves if we believe that! And when the parents who have heard about these experiences meet up with those other community members who don't think we're doing our jobs, then those who don't know suddenly have "proof positive" that their beliefs are validated and, voila, case closed, one more reason for them to vote against the next tax referendum in support of public education. The "truth" is out there and they just "found" it!

ABOUT THOSE "THEY DIDN'T DO ANYTHING" CLAIMS

Do school personnel really ignore bullying and teasing when they see it? Not for the most part. Now, let's try to determine what that "for the most part" means. For the most part, educators make a good-faith effort to stop those intimidating behaviors they see, especially those so blatant that they cannot ignore them. Unfortunately, however, we also know that those kinds of behaviors do not always happen right under our noses. We know that they are ongoing in Kid World all around us during the school day. And what we educators think we are doing and what the kids tell their parents may be two different things. Craig, Henderson, and Murphy (2000) point out that prospective teachers' attitudes about bullying affect the likelihood of their intervention and that there exists a difference between teachers' and students' perceptions of the effectiveness of those interventions.

> *When I talk to them up at the school, they just don't get it. They think I'm the one with the problem, or that it's my son's fault and that his learning disability makes it okay for kids to pick on him because he's different.*
>
> Mother of a ninth-grade boy

That, then, becomes the crux of the problem for parents in their perceptions of how school personnel respond to bullying. Parents may know full well that staff do what they "have to" to stop the most flagrant intimidating behaviors in their children's schools, but *they don't feel as if the effort is consistent* or that we go that "extra mile" to do the *follow-up* and *prevention* that are always necessary to stop the next episode from happening. Is this a fair perception of educators? Not always—but sometimes. Certainly some communities and schools take the problem of intimidation very seriously and make major efforts to reduce overall tensions within the student body. They embed a culture of respect for everyone within the hallways of the school. However, there are also schools in which the problem is pooh-poohed, if not outright denied. Though not enough, even a halfhearted effort to address the problem is better than outright denial.

The problem for school personnel about those "they didn't do anything" rumors is that one or more vocal parents within a community can make the claim stick, be it true or not, and woe be unto the staff members and schools of those parents who know how to get their voices heard. Such claims can do a lot of damage to all staff members within the school because they are tarred with the same brush as uncaring or negligent about safeguarding the children under their care. It is just as unfair for faculty to be maligned as uncaring or lazy about responding to bullying in their schools as it is for students to have to put up with being mistreated when such rumors are, indeed, fact. Nobody wins in that kind of situation.

DOCUMENTING THE FACTS ON SCHOOL INTERVENTIONS

One of the most effective ways to respond to parents' concerns about an ineffective response to bullying is to have the facts that contradict that claim and to provide evidence of exactly what *has* been done to address the problem. Evidence might include (1) an overall school effort to combat bullying (e.g., an embedded character education curriculum focusing on kindness at the elementary level or a schoolwide focus at the secondary level on tolerance and understanding differences); (2) examples of how school personnel have addressed the misbehaviors of students involved in bullying (while protecting student confidentially, of course); and (3) best of all, specific examples of how staff have responded to the mistreatment directed at the parent's child. It is hard for parents to argue against the good-faith efforts made by the school on behalf of their child, even if the efforts are not providing the kind of responses that the parents wish.

At the end of the chapter, Figure 3.1 gives an example of a letter crafted to respond to parents' concerns and repeated claims that school staff members were ignoring the mistreatment of their child. (As with any template, educators should vet this sample with administration to ensure that it follows district protocol.) Notice the way the letter addresses the parents' concerns directly and to the point. A sound letter to parents regarding their concerns about bullying directed at their child incorporates the following six principles.

1. Respectfully Addresses the Parents' Concern About the Child

The letter must exemplify the highest levels of respect for a parent's concern about whatever misbehavior has caused a negative learning experience for the child—even if the child is a part of the problem and the parent has a tendency to be difficult in communications with the school. Children can misbehave and parents can be difficult, but educators must maintain the high road in dealing with them at all times. Doing so increases the likelihood that the doors of communication will remain open. Being demeaning or belittling or taking an arrogant attitude toward parents only further convinces them that we have uncaring sentiments toward children in general; for what not to write (and certainly *not* say!), see the following actual quote.

> *Frankly, I don't really care what happens to the little s——. He causes all the problems around here and if he has to spend the rest of his life in jail, that's all right by me.*
>
> Middle school principal

This is not to say that we should tolerate abuse from parents—absolutely not. However, we must strive to maintain a professional and mature demeanor at all times in dealing with parents when they have real concerns about their children, be those concerns legitimate or not. Frustrated parents are far more likely to seek legal counsel about any number of aggravations (and more likely to win in court) if they can prove they received a dismissive response from school personnel.

2. Identifies Who Has Been Involved in the Remediation Efforts

Although the best solutions are often the simplest and involve the fewest people, evidence of multiple consultations to resolve complicated problems can reduce parent impressions about an uncaring attitude among staff. In the instance described in the letter, no fewer than five school staff members—six if one counts the superintendent—were involved in meetings about the student during the two-week period. This does not include the number of staff who also met with the aggressors' parents. Clearly, the staff at this elementary school are working hard to address the issue. All of the teachers who observed the incidents are involved, and the school counselor has been pressed into service as a mediator for both the parents and the students. There is no shortage of school staff involvement here.

3. Documents the Specific Efforts, With Dates, Made to Remediate the Situation

This section is probably the most important part of the letter, especially in demonstrating to parents that, indeed, the school has made efforts to reach out to the student targeted by bullies to make the child's school experience more welcoming than it has been. The staff had no fewer than four meetings with the student who was abused by her peers before she withdrew from school. There were 10 specific student-parent-staff contacts of some kind—actually one each day—during the past two school weeks in efforts to resolve the issue with this one family. Remember, the letter does not include information about contacts with other students and their families. How much time has been consumed by school staff just dealing with this situation over the past two weeks? A lot. That is what happens when bullying occurs and the dominoes start to fall in the face of a valid school response.

4. Protects the Confidentiality of All Students Involved as May Be Required by State Statutes

> *I spoke with his teachers. I spoke with the principal. I even went to the superintendent. They just didn't get it—none of them. As long as it was something that affected only one kid, they just didn't care. But I care. My kid cares, and my kid is the one that's being hurt not only by the jerks that push him around, but also by the whole school district who just thinks that this stuff is nothing to be concerned about.*
>
> Mother of an eighth-grade boy

States vary in regard to what they allow educators to do and not do in communicating with parents about their interactions with other students. State confidentiality laws are especially vexing to parents when they want to know how other children have been held accountable for harming their child. Parents want to know if the offending party has been punished enough to make sure that it won't happen again—at least not to their child. In all honesty, parents often may have a little revenge motive in wanting a bully to be punished by the school because they can't do it themselves. Oh, and trust me on this one, there are plenty of parents who would more than gladly take matters into their own hands if they thought they could get away with it. *Under no circumstance can school personnel ever be involved in any type of sharing of information that would put another child, or that child's family members, at risk.* It may sound absurd that anyone would do this, but I am aware of instances in which school personnel have intimated that perhaps the best way to solve the problem of bullying is for the parent to become the intimidator of the family of the bully, or even worse, intimidate the bully directly. We've all seen the bus surveillance tapes of the parents who came onboard and attacked children who were supposed to be the aggressors against their child. Some parents—thankfully, though, very few—are fully capable of acting foolishly on their own without our help.

Parents do have the right to know that those who harm their child are properly held accountable, but they also need to understand that accountability and punishment are not necessarily the same things. Then there's that little pesky problem with the law and confidentiality. Depending on the state in which one lives, it may be illegal for school personnel to provide *any* kind of information to parents about other students, even those who may have transgressed in some fashion against their child, without parental approval of the offending child. That is not to say that the parents of a victimized child will not already know who did what from information received from their own child, but school personnel are *strongly advised* to know the laws related to what they can and cannot say during a parent-teacher conference regarding other children. The law even covers off-the-cuff remarks made when responding to a parent's comment about other children.

5. *Honestly Acknowledges What the School Can and Cannot Do*
School personnel cannot provide a 100% ironclad guarantee that a child will be safe from harm in every instance while at school, as evidenced by the number of bloody noses and skinned knees that occur from accidents on the playground. However, school personnel can and better be able to give a 100% guarantee to parents that they are *committed to* and will *try to do everything humanly possible* to protect a child while under school supervision. It is not reasonable for parents to believe that school personnel will provide personal tutoring and protection for their child throughout the school day, but it is a responsibility of the school to ensure that it constantly updates its efforts to maintain and increase school security. A large part of ensuring a safe school comes from designing plans and curricula for bullying prevention. After all, we have ample documented cases that bullying leads to a plague of ills among our children, the worst examples being murder and suicide when victims turn their torment outward or inward.

6. *Encourages an Open and Continued Dialogue With the Parents*
One of the biggest complaints that parents have of teacher response to their concerns about the bullying of their child is that, when the discussions reach a critical point, school personnel dig in and declare that the parent is "overreacting" or is "difficult." Let us not fool ourselves. Such labels are School Speak code words for "nuts," as in "That man's *crazy!*" It is much easier for us to deny the legitimacy of a parent's claim if we can minimize the concerns as coming from an irrational, overly emotional person. Of course, parents who have their ducks in a row are sometimes perceived as a direct threat to educator credibility, especially if they are *right* about school negligence when it comes to addressing the intimidation of their child.

The quickest way to slam the door of open communication shut is to make the person who is coming to us for help feel ridiculed and ignored. When that happens, frustration grows, tempers rise, and parents do one of two things—either go away (which sometimes may be what we would actually *prefer!*) or, if they know how to work the system and have the time and resources to follow through, go public with their concerns and, in a worst-case scenario, get a lawyer and sue the school.

> *The reason we were able to solve it was because the school counselor was the one willing to do the heavy lifting and convince his teachers and the principal that there really was a problem with bullying during the lunch hour. It didn't make any difference to me who did it—it could have been the janitor for all I cared—as long as somebody at the school knew that we were telling the truth about what was going on and was willing to help us be heard.*
>
> Father of a ninth-grade boy

School personnel should *never*, unless threatened, be the ones who encourage the cutting off of communications about difficult subjects. We must be the ones who stick to that higher road, no matter how bumpy it gets with a truly difficult parent. Keeping the door of communication open always increases the likelihood that, after a time of calmer consideration by all parties involved and distance from the original event, a parent will be able to return to school personnel with more insight into the total picture than their original only-focused-on-my-child mission.

We've now looked at some of the reasons why parents may be skeptical about our services when it comes to responding to the bullying they believe their child is receiving. We've seen the importance of documenting exactly what we've done so that we can show the parents our hard work and efforts to make things better. What we have to do now is look at some of the ways in which we can improve communication with parents when we actually get to discuss the problem face-to-face. Although written communication is acceptable, we can often avoid many of the pitfalls and achieve the outcomes exemplified in Figure 3.1 by talking directly with parents about how we need their assistance and how they are part of the solution. So, let's go on to Chapter 4 and learn some techniques for engaging those parents whose child is bullied.

Figure 3.1   Sample Letter to Parents Regarding Concerns About Perceptions That the School Is Failing to Address the Bullying of Their Child

Mr. and Mrs. Concerned Parent
3215 Crikey Highway
Bulldog, Arizona

Mr. and Mrs. Parent,

We received your letter regarding your concerns about the way that our school has handled the treatment by peers of your daughter, Melissa. As we have stated previously, we share your concerns. This letter is in response to your request of March 23rd, 2007, for more formal documentation of our efforts on behalf of Melissa.

To date, several members of our staff have met with one or both of you regarding this matter three times. It is clear that you are frustrated by what you feel is a lack of effective response on our staff's part to address perceived mistreatment of Melissa by her peers. After my last conversation with you, we gathered all of those staff who have been involved in the matter at some point over the past few weeks to ensure that we are all on the same page in our responses to your and Melissa's concerns. That meeting included Mr. Carlo Rogeria, school counselor; Mr. Aris Totle, Melissa's primary teacher; Ms. Patricia Metheny, the music instructor; Ms. Mary Thon, the P.E. instructor; and me.

As we have all shared with you, either in individual or group meetings, we have worked hard to respond to the problems Melissa has experienced in recent weeks. Specifically, we have done the following:

> March 12th: Met with Melissa and the individuals involved immediately after the incident on the playground where Melissa was hit with a rock (Mr. Totle and Mr. Rogeria).

> March 13th: Met with Mrs. Parent to discuss the incident (Mr. Totle and me). Met with Melissa to see how she was handling the initial incident (Mr. Rogeria).

> March 14th: A second incident in the music room bathroom area occurred with the same girls involved in the March 12th incident. Met with those who approached Melissa in the bathroom (Ms. Metheny and me). Met with Melissa (Mr. Rogeria and me). Conferences scheduled with the parents of the girls involved in the second incident over the next two days.

> March 15th–16th: Met with the parents of the girls involved in both incidents (Mr. Rogeria and me). Met with Melissa on March 15th to determine what she might need to continue to succeed in school (Mr. Rogeria).

> March 16th: Met with Mr. Parent to discuss concerns regarding both incidents.

> March 19th: Melissa complained of feeling sick in P.E. Ms. Thon released Melissa to call her mother for pickup.

> March 20th: Melissa absent. I talked with Mrs. Parent over the phone about her concerns that Melissa did not want to come to school because of the two incidents.

> March 21st: Melissa absent again. Mr. Rogeria called Mrs. Parent to inquire about Melissa.

> March 22nd: Mrs. Parent called the superintendent's office to indicate her dissatisfaction with the school's response. I personally met with the superintendent to review the issue that day.

> March 23rd: Mr. Parent called and requested documentation of what the school had done to address the issue and indicated that Melissa would likely not return unless we could guarantee that further mistreatment would not occur. Staff involved with knowledge of Melissa's concerns called me after school and we talked for one hour to discuss options.

While state law prevents us from discussing with you the other students involved, I can say that we always address such behaviors with discipline and corrective actions to decrease the likelihood that they will occur again.

As much as I would like to guarantee that Melissa will not receive further teasing or bullying in the future, I cannot do so. We keep close supervision over all our students but, unfortunately, there may be times when children misbehave and we are unable to prevent it. You do need to know that we follow a Kindness Curriculum within all the elementary schools in the Bulldog District. A part of that curriculum is that teachers,

(Continued)

(Continued)

as well as students, all pledge to address bullying and teasing when it occurs. What I think is safe to say is that you have our continued commitment to do whatever we can to safeguard our students while they are under our care. That is a promise that all school staff agree to uphold during their tenure with us.

Melissa's experience this year has been sad for all of us—we, too, do not like what has occurred and, as you can see, have made a major effort to prevent it from happening again, not only to Melissa, but to all students here at Little Bulldog Elementary. We want Melissa back and hope that we all can work together to make that happen. Please do not hesitate to contact me to further discuss this matter at your convenience.

Sincerely,

Seymour Skinner
Principal

NOTES

1. See Table 10, p. 45, of the 2006 PDK/G Poll survey.

2. See Table 27, p. 48, of the 2006 PDK/G Poll survey.

3. See p. v and Table 1 (Appendix B) of *Student Reports of Bullying: Results From the 2001 School Crime Supplement to the National Crime Victimization Survey* (DeVoe & Kaffenberger, 2005).

4. Ibid., p. vi, Figure 2 (p. 6), and Table 1 (Appendix B).

5. Ibid., p. vi and Table 2 (Appendix B).

6. Ibid., p. vi and Table 3 (Appendix B).

7. Ibid., p. vii, Figure 6 (p. 12), and Table 6 (Appendix B).

8. Ibid., p. vii, Figure 7 (p. 13), and Table 7 (Appendix B).

CHAPTER FOUR

How to Talk With Parents Whose Children Are Bullied

Now that we know some of the things that parents think and say about how educators respond to bullying and teasing of their children, let's look at some strategies and tactics to address their concerns directly when we get them to pay us a visit at school.

Let's face reality. As we saw in Chapter 3, parents whose children receive peer-on-peer abuse in school may not think educators are doing enough to solve the problem. Whether true or not—and we hope it is not—perception has a tendency to become reality for those who choose to live there. So, what can we do to be helpful to those parents who may well be coming into our schools distrustful of our services?

First, let us not be shy about addressing the problem head-on. There is no need to dance around the truth. Chances are pretty high that intimidation of some sort *is* occurring in *your* school! We know it's happening in other schools on a steady basis (see the article by Nansel et al. [2001] in the *Journal of the American Medical Association* for additional results of another nationwide study on the subject), so why should we assume that it happens only in those "other" schools and not ours? Reality check: kids have many behaviors that are universal, regardless of family or cultural background, and one of those universals is an effort to establish rank among peers. This effort is commonly exemplified through behaviors that attempt to dominate others—whether physically, verbally, or psychologically—within the immediate peer group. It is less evident during the preschool and early elementary years, explodes in the late elementary and middle school grades, and declines with age (see DeVoe & Kaffenberger, 2005, Figure 2). So, let us dispense with the silly notion that "that kind of stuff doesn't happen here in our school," unless, of course, all students have their own adult chaperone from the time they hit the school domain until the time they are personally escorted back home each afternoon. Intimidation has occurred in your school, it does occur, and only with constant vigilance will its likelihood be reduced in the future.

Second, by showing a willingness to work toward solving the problem, or at the very least, investigate a parent's concerns, educators are keeping open the door of communication and increasing the likelihood of working in an **alliance mode** toward seeking solutions. That alliance mode is central to the focus of this effort. An alliance mode assumes a **partnership** between school and home. It denotes a minimum of two parties working toward a similar goal. In that alliance, *each partner agrees to certain responsibilities* that are understood from the get-go: supervisory personnel in educational settings will take care of the educational setting arena, and parents will take care of the home environment. In a perfect world, the children involved form the third leg of the partnership alliance, but we have to assume that children and adolescents who are being abused may not have the resources to perform at the level of an equal partner—at least, not yet. Ultimately, one goal is to stabilize the situation so that the child who is victimized has the time and chance to learn the behaviors to avoid or be able to fend off intimidation from those peers creating the problem. Simultaneously, there must also be an effort to partner with the parents of the peers who are creating the problem, but that's the topic for the next chapter. In essence, the alliance between parents and school staff "bookends" the situation to provide order out of what is now chaos.

PARENTS OF BULLIED CHILDREN: THE TWO CAMPS

Parents of children who are bullied are likely to fall into one of two camps: those who are *actively involved* in their child's educational experience and those who are *less involved* in their child's school activities. Both groups bring advantages and disadvantages with them into the alliance partnership.

Parents who come to school personnel with concerns about their child being intimidated and who have experience dealing with us about all things school related are most likely more adept at understanding the ins and outs of parent-teacher interactions. Most likely, they have had a reasonable amount of positive interactions with school personnel on any number of activities, enough to keep them coming back for more. Parents who are "frequent flyers" at the school may be there because they see the school as responsive to their concerns. They may even understand some of the "eduspeak" that educators use on a regular basis, but which makes most parents' eyes glaze over when used in conferences. Then, of course, there are also those frequent flyers whom we cattily refer to as "helicopter parents" because they "hover" over every aspect of their child's life and interfere with the child's ability to experience life independently. Helicopter parents present special problems when working toward a solution of *any* magnitude with their children because they tend to try to solve the problem themselves.

We have to be particularly aware of the parents in the second camp, those who are less involved in their child's educational experience. What is it that is preventing them from having anything but minimal contact with those who are educating their child? Many such parents view school as not responsive to their concerns. Although this may or may not be the reality, remember that perception tends to become reality when we begin behaving as if it is. Sometimes parents are hesitant to come to seek school personnel's advice because they had poor experiences themselves during their school years. Many other parents never receive an "invitation" to come to their children's school unless something is "wrong," the child has "messed up," is failing, or is misbehaving, or something else is deemed "not right" about their child's educational progress. Who wants to seek help from the people who deem their child as somehow "unfit"? How welcome do we make these parents feel if the only time we send a note home is when there is some kind of "problem"? And I haven't even touched on those groups who are unfamiliar with the educational system of a country, such as immigrant parents who may not speak the predominant language and who may well be spending every waking hour attempting to provide food, clothing, and shelter for their children at entry-level minimum-wage employment. Immigrants often revere school personnel or are intimidated by us by virtue of the very position we hold. Predominant cultures tend to forget how important education is to those groups just starting out in this country.

WORKING WITH THE ACTIVELY INVOLVED PARENT

Actively involved parents will be more than willing to engage school personnel in expressing their concerns about the mistreatment of their children. Good for them, as long as their approach is respectful and appropriate. If not, we may have to help them understand from the outset that nobody wins when partners who are supposed to be working together yell every time they sit down to discuss an issue.

Case Study: An Actively Involved Parent

Jolene Campi is the mother of a fourth-grade girl, Hannah. Hannah has recently reported to her mother that she has been shunned by her former friends after a sleepover a few weekends ago. Hannah's revelation came about after Ms. Campi discovered her daughter crying in her room last Sunday night. As she opened up to her mother, Hannah revealed that her friends not only had been excluding her from their normal peer group activities but had also begun passing notes around school saying demeaning things about her and encouraging other fourth graders to exclude Hannah from activities, both in and out of school. Ms. Campi has been an active parent in Hannah's school, but she has a tendency to be somewhat emotional too, and when she appeared at Hannah's teacher's door after school on Monday, she was both angry and flustered about the whole situation. The teacher, Mr. Hanson, did not know that she was coming.

Parent [P]:   *Mr. Hanson, I just have to talk to you today.*

Teacher [T]:   *Ms. Campi, I didn't know you were coming. Did we have an appointment?*

[P]:   *No, but this is something that can't wait. Have you got a few minutes?*

[T]:   *In all honesty, that's really all I have. I've got a personal commitment scheduled this afternoon that I have to leave for in 15 minutes, so I can't promise that we can spend as much time on it as necessary today. We may need to reschedule. So, in a nutshell, what's going on?*

[P]:   *It's Hannah, of course. I just found out this weekend that she's been being bullied here at school by her so-called friends, and I think it's something that you need to know about and help stop.*

[T]:   *Well, at the outset let me tell you that we don't want anyone to be mistreated here at Frederick Perls Elementary, but that bullying and teasing are quite hard to prevent all the time. Now that you mention it, I have noticed that she's been quieter than normal the last week or so. What has been happening?*

[P]:   [Ms. Campi explains what she discovered from Hannah the previous night and gives several of the notes about Hannah to Mr. Hanson.]

[T]:   [Mr. Hanson reads the notes. They are clearly intended to harm Hannah's reputation in school.] *This is clearly not good, and I thank you for sharing this information with me. I do need to know and we will begin to work on this first thing tomorrow. But for now, like I said, I have to get to this previously scheduled appointment. Let me take these notes with me, and I'll call you back tomorrow to talk further about this. I'm really sorry that all of this is happening and that I can't talk more right now.*

[P]:   *You promise?*

[T]:   *Jolene, I think you know me well enough to know that I don't like my little chickens to have anything but the best time they can have in school because that increases the likelihood that they'll learn more. This kind of silliness hurts everyone, so yes, you know I'll get back to you first thing tomorrow. I might also be able to come up with some ideas tonight that will prove helpful. Now, if you'll excuse me, I have to get to this appointment.*

[P]:   *Maybe I should talk to the principal if you don't have the time to mess with this.*

[T]:   *Jolene, I do have time to mess with this, but I can't right now until tomorrow because, as I said, I have a previously scheduled appointment. You are free to talk to the principal anytime you feel you need to. I know that Ms. Donovan will be as concerned about this as I am, but I also know that Ms. Donovan will end up coming back down here to me first thing tomorrow to discuss this with me, which is exactly what I am going to do myself—go see her, too.*

[P]:   *I'm just concerned, that's all. Hannah is very upset.*

[T]:   *And I'm concerned too; that's why first thing tomorrow morning I'll have some better handle on this after I can think about it tonight. But, again, if you want to go see Ms. Donovan, you are certainly free to do so.*

[P]:   *Oh, I guess I'll wait.*

[T]:   *I'll call you first thing tomorrow morning. Promise!*

Let's analyze what occurred in this exchange between the parent and the teacher.

The parent appeared unannounced at the teacher's door after school in an agitated state—not angry, just excited. Although Ms. Campi wanted immediate attention and resolution of the problem, she was at least reasonable when Mr. Hanson explained to her that he could not provide her with the amount of attention both she and he would have preferred. The teacher responded fairly and honestly under the circumstances by setting a **boundary** for the conditions of the talk that afternoon. Educators have lives too, and a parent's unscheduled appearance about a child's problem—unless that problem is life threatening, which, in this case, after reviewing the notes, Mr. Hanson could see that it was not—often cannot be addressed properly on the whim of the anxious parent. The teacher was *firm, fair, friendly*, and *professional* when setting the boundary. He *clearly stated the reasons* that prevented him from staying longer at that particular time.

The parent challenged the teacher with a low-level threat to go immediately to the principal with her concerns. In this instance, Ms. Campi's thoughts about going to the principal were more likely motivated by her eagerness for "somebody to do something now to save my baby!" than a desire to cause trouble for Mr. Hanson. The teacher's response to the parent's thinking-out-loud comment of going to see the principal was to *show a cooperative willingness to help* the parent do what she thought necessary under the current conditions. Mr. Hanson was *not defensive*, nor did he show alarm at the prospect of having a parent request the same kind of assistance from the principal. This is the way things should be. Teachers should not fear a parent's desire or threat to see the principal about difficult issues, especially when there is a protocol in place for responding to such instances. Clearly, the teacher knows what will happen if the parent goes to the principal—the principal will return to the teacher to gather more facts about the situation in order to make the most effective decision possible on behalf of all involved. Fear has no place in education, whether between teachers and students, teachers and parents, or teachers and administrators.

In this instance, a good relationship already exists between the teacher and the parent and it yields a positive result. Mr. Hanson has had multiple interactions with the Campi family, particularly with Ms. Campi, about Hannah's educational progress. When questioned about the likelihood of his follow-through on the mother's concerns, Mr. Hanson used his responses to her previous concerns to remind her that his track record was one that could be counted on. He told her that there was no reason to assume that the future would be any different, even though he did not have the time right then to delve more deeply into the matter. The teacher's response to the parent was not defensive. Mr. Hanson might have wanted to say, "What do you mean by asking me if I'll get back to you on this and start working on it first thing tomorrow?!? You show up here unannounced when I've got a long-standing appointment to go to with my wife for an ultrasound on our first child and you want me to drop everything to deal with this issue right now!?! And, besides that, haven't I always done what I said I would do to help Hannah out with stuff?!? You gottalottanerve!" Although we may *think* these things (and, in all honesty, we all know that there are times that we do!), it's a tad bit wise to make certain that we keep our thoughts to ourselves if we plan to keep those doors of communication open.

In fact, everything in this dialogue was designed to *keep the communication lines open.* Mr. Hanson indicated that he would get back to Ms. Campi the next morning. (Although teachers certainly have the option to contact a parent after school hours on their own time, that is a personal decision that all educators have to make for themselves. Too often educators do not set enough personal boundaries when away from school because of the workload demands or because of their genuine concern for their kids; hence, they end up being "on duty" 24/7, a surefire recipe for burnout.) He also indicated that Ms. Campi was free to talk to the principal if she so chose. At no point in the interaction did the teacher respond in a negative way so that communication would be hindered. The parent was given every opportunity to ask questions and act on her concerns, regardless of what the teacher might have really thought or known about the protocol for handling parent concerns in the school. He informed the parent of what was likely to happen with her inquiry with the principal. There were *no hidden agendas* in play by the teacher, even though the parent continued to push for immediate resolution of the issue.

Mr. Hanson's next day was a busy one. The previous night he recognized the handwriting in the notes as some of the other girls in his classroom and knew everything that he needed to do to start dealing with that aspect of the intervention. He called Ms. Campi, as promised, early the next morning from school to set up an appointment for that same afternoon. Here is how their conversation went in that conference:

[T]: *Ms. Campi, thanks so much for coming back today. I'm really sorry that we couldn't talk more yesterday, but I'm sure you understand.*

[P]: *So what did you find out?*

[T]: *As I mentioned over the phone, the principal and I met today briefly to discuss this matter and we both talked with the students involved—*

[P]: *Who were they? I know a couple of them, but what about the others.*

[T]: *I'm not allowed to discuss other students by name because of school laws. I would encourage you to ask Hannah about that. What I was saying was—*

[P]: *What do you mean you can't tell me who they are? Don't I have a right to know who's picking on my child?*

[T]: *It must sound strange and I'm sure it's frustrating for you, but the law is very clear that teachers are not to discuss student discipline matters with parents unless it's their child.*

[P]: *That's not right.*

[T]:   *I'm not agreeing or disagreeing with you, Ms. Campi. I'm just following the law.*

[P]:   *Well, I'll just talk to Ms. Donovan about this and see if she'll tell me.*

[T]:   *You're always free to do whatever you think is necessary, and I'll even check with Ms. Donovan when we're through here to see if she's available to talk with you. But I would really like to share with you what I did in response to the concerns you brought me yesterday.*

[P]:   *Okay, okay. I'm just upset, that's all.*

[T]:   *I can tell and I'm trying to help, believe me.* [Mr. Hanson then proceeds to share the details of what he has been able to discern and do so far. He has talked not only with Ms. Donovan, the principal, but also with Mr. Lazarus, the school counselor. The three of them have come up with a plan to address both the girls who did the bullying and Hannah's needs as well.] *So, that's where we are as far as what we're doing here at school. Do you have any questions?*

[P]:   *What are you exactly going to do for Hannah?*

[T]:   *Let me go over that again, because not only are we going to be working with Hannah here to make sure that she knows she's safe here and that school is as fun a place as it can be for her, but we also are going to need your help too.*

[P]:   *My help? Why my help?*

[T]:   *Because we can do only so much here without parent help. You have been so actively involved in Hannah's schooling to this point. You know how important it is for children to know that their parents support them in their schoolwork. It's also important that children know that their parents support them when they are having trouble in other areas too. Kids need to know that we want to hear about their lives not just when things are going great, but also when things aren't going so well either. If Hannah had told any of us sooner that this stuff was going on, we all would have been more likely to have headed off some of the mean things that have been directed toward her.*

[P]:   *So what am I supposed to do?*

[T]:   *First of all, Hannah needs to know that you are proud of her for sharing the information with you about her mistreatment. Right now, she feels badly about that because she knows that you're upset and—*

[P]:   *I have a right to be upset!*

[T]:   *Parents are fully entitled to want the best for their child. But we also do not want Hannah to think that just because she shared something with you that upset you, she can't talk to you in the future. We want her to share more about these kinds of incidents, not less.*

[P]:   *I never thought my getting upset might send her the message that I don't want her to talk to me about things like this when she needs to.*

[T]:   *Well, kids pick up all sorts of messages from us when we're upset, and they're not always the ones we want them to remember.*

Let's stop for a moment and analyze the conference to this point.

The teacher showed *good faith* and was *accountable* for what he had promised he would do the previous day—Mr. Hanson did, indeed, *follow up* exactly as he said he would. He shared that information with the parent. Although he was limited in full disclosure of all the particulars because of state statutes (see Chapter 3), he nonetheless shared all that he could and *encouraged the parent to continue the discussion with her child* to fill in that information that he could not divulge. In doing so, Mr. Hanson was setting the stage for the parent's role in what was about to transpire—bringing the parent into the parent-teacher partnership.

Even though Ms. Campi interrupted him several times, the teacher *stayed focused on the issue* at hand. Staying focused is extremely critical when discussing difficult issues. Emotions have a tendency to sidetrack any negotiation because they override rational thought at a primitive level. If you yell at me, I grow alarmed. I may feel threatened. My evolutionary DNA tells me that something is amiss. If I feel threatened, then I may be in danger, and when the body goes into danger mode, thinking shuts down. I make plans to do one of three things: fight, flee, or freeze. That's what we humans are programmed to do in dangerous situations so that we can outsmart that saber-toothed tiger about to pounce on us. We react primally; we don't think.

That's why so many parent-educator discussions go astray. Heightened emotions give way to gut-level reactions. Things get said that don't get vetted at a conscious level. Although it is not okay for parents to be rude and disrespectful (and educators are fully entitled to set the boundaries about such behaviors when they occur), teachers always have to be the ones who are mindful about what it is that comes out of their mouths. *We* have to be the wise ones in times of chaos.

Mr. Hanson stayed focused throughout this exchange with Ms. Campi. He continually referred to the issue under discussion. He did not argue when the parent challenged him about her seeking the identities of the culprits who were harassing her daughter from the principal or when she indicated how upset she was with the entire matter. Those interjections were **distracters** to the issue at hand. Distracters may or may not be relevant to a discussion—that is a decision that an educator will have to determine on the spot. If relevant, then perhaps it is not a distracter so much as just another fact to add to the mix. Usually, of course, a distracter is not relevant and tends to emerge from that emotional level, which, as previously noted, encourages us to respond in kind. Again, the key is always to stay focused. What we want to avoid is anything that puts up additional barriers to keeping the doors of communication open. Distracters do just that.

Now, back to our conference:

[P]:   *So, what is it that you want me to do?*

[T]:   *First and foremost, we need you to share with Hannah that you support our efforts here at school to make it a safe place for her.*

[P]: *But what if I don't agree with that?*

[T]: *Then, by all means, don't say anything that you don't believe is accurate. But I hope that by the time we end our meeting today that you'll feel as if we really do have something to offer Hannah—*

[P]: *Oh, I didn't mean that you don't!*

[T]: *Thanks. I know we do too. What we're trying to do is help Hannah understand that we're all in this together—her teachers, her parents, her peers—and that we're all going to be working hard to improve the situation for everyone. If we can convince her that we're a team, it might go a long way toward improving her over-all mood right now that school's not a happy place for her.*

[P]: [Thinks about what is being said.]

[T]: *If you can let Hannah know that we all want to know when things are not going well for her, that while we can't solve all her problems, some of them we can certainly help with in some ways, I think that that might help her share information about something like this in the future.*

[P]: *Let's hope that there isn't another episode like this in the future.*

[T]: *I agree, but we have to be realistic. Kids do hurtful things to their peers. Sometimes they don't even know it, other times they do. That's just a fact of life in Kid World. But we want Hannah to know that we are here, both at school and at home, to help make things better if we can. Now, let me take you down to Ms. Donovan's office to see if she's there.*

[P]: *I'm not sure I need to go now. I think I get the plan.*

[T]: *Well, we'll do what you feel most comfortable doing, but I'm more than willing to go with you down to see Ms. Donovan if you still feel you need to. And I would also like to talk to you about this later this week to see how things are going at home and to update you with what we're seeing here at school. Feel free to call me too if you need to. I'll get back to you when I can on prep or before or after school if my schedule allows it.*

The conference between the parent and teacher *ends on a positive note*. The teacher offers to help the parent meet with the principal, if she still wants to do so. There is a *short-term plan* to engage the *parent as a participant* in the alliance mode. It has been explained to the parent why her involvement is important, both for the school and in the home. This is a *team effort*. Everybody is involved. Everybody wins when the child wins.

WORKING WITH THE LESS ACTIVELY INVOLVED PARENT

Less actively involved parents pose different challenges. Their contact with the school is limited for some reason. Exactly what that reason is may or may not have anything to do with school personnel, but at the very least, educators must not provide additional barriers to those parents that would decrease further educator-parent interaction.

As previously mentioned, less actively involved parents may have had negative contacts with school personnel in the past. If that is the case, they are likely to find parent-educator conferences difficult. This is especially true if the only time a parent has been inside a child's school is when the child was involved in some kind of mischief that required parental involvement in order to avoid a suspension or other form of harsh discipline.

Case Study: A Less Actively Involved Parent

Enrico Rojas is the father of 13-year-old Felipe. Felipe has recently been skipping his last period class in seventh-grade gym. His teacher, Ms. Sutterfield, caught Felipe recently and, in questioning him about what was occurring, discovered that he had been skipping her class because his classmates had been making fun of him. Ms. Sutterfield called Felipe's home and talked to his mother, who then referred the matter to Mr. Rojas. Neither of Felipe's parents has ever attended a school conference on his behalf. Felipe is the oldest child in his family. When Mr. Rojas met with Ms. Sutterfield, it was immediately apparent that the situation was awkward for him.

Teacher [T]:   *Mr. Rojas, welcome to our school. I'm Ms. Sutterfield, Felipe's gym teacher. Thank you for coming today. Please, have a seat.*

Parent [P]:   [Smiles and nods, but says nothing.]

[T]:   *I'm sorry that we're here to discuss Felipe's absences in gym today. I wish that we were here to discuss something else.*

[P]:   [Nods, smiles again. It is clear that Mr. Rojas is uncertain exactly what his role should be in the situation.]

[T]:   *Please feel free to ask any questions that you may want to ask as we go along. I want to you know that Felipe's skipping my class is not what I'm most concerned about. I think we have an understanding with him here at school as to why he was doing that and I don't think that it will be a problem again in the future.*

[P]:   *We talked with him about this last night. He told us about the boys picking on him and that he felt embarrassed to go to gym as long as they were doing this. We also told him that it was wrong to skip class.*

[T]:   *Felipe told me today about your talk last night. We appreciate your helping us on this, and that's a part of what I want to talk with you about today. [Ms. Sutterfield provides as many details as possible about what the school has done with the individuals who were bullying Felipe.] I want you to know that I personally apologize for not figuring out what was going on sooner with your son. All I knew was that he wasn't showing up in gym, and until I happened to overhear a conversation among the boys who were creating the problem by forcing Felipe to hide behind the gym until the buses came, I presumed that he was leaving campus and so all I did was report him*

> *absent to the office. I'm really glad that we were able to figure out what was going on and that we now have been able to stop that behavior from occurring again. Do you have any questions at this point, Mr. Rojas?*

Let's do the analysis of what is happening up to this point with Mr. Rojas. The teacher opens the conversation and conveys tremendous *respect for the parent.* Ms. Sutterfield immediately perceives the awkwardness of the situation and *responds to the cultural variables* of the interaction. Her goal is to *make the discussion as nonthreatening as possible* for the parent because she recognizes that this is the first time Mr. Rojas has been at his son's school. The teacher *includes many opportunities and much encouragement for the parent to ask questions.* She understands that, because the situation is awkward for Mr. Rojas, it will likely take several minutes and invitations before he may feel comfortable asking a question. That is because the parent views the teacher as superior and more knowledgeable in the interaction and, as a matter of deference to the teacher, may think that asking questions is a sign of challenge or disrespect to authority. This deference could either be cultural or stem from a lack of familiarity with how a teacher-parent conference is supposed to work. Either way, Ms. Sutterfield is wise to make every effort to ensure that the parent has ample opportunity to ask questions and know that it is safe to do so.

Now, back to the conference:

[P]:   *What will be Felipe's punishment for skipping class?*

[T]:   *Actually, not much because of the circumstances. I talked to him about the mistake and shared with him that he will have to make up the assignments that he missed. We also talked about what to do the next time something like this comes up.*

[P]:   *But he was wrong to skip. We don't teach him to do that.*

[T]:   *I believe you. I also believe that Felipe was mistreated by his classmates and that his skipping class was not what he really wanted to do, but that he didn't know that he could tell me or another teacher here at school to help get the teasing stopped. That's why I spoke with the principal about letting me handle the incident instead of making the matter worse for Felipe by suspending him for skipping class, which, in all honesty, wouldn't do anyone any good under the circumstances.*

[P]:   *Thank you. We did punish him at home for skipping class.*

[T]:   *May I ask what you did?*

[P]:   *He's grounded all week from television and video games. He can use the computer only if it has something to do with his homework.*

[T]:   *Well, that's certainly your call on how you want to handle him at home. But I want you to know that I believe that he won't do that again and that he wouldn't have this time if the bullying hadn't been taking place.*

[P]:   *As long as you know that we don't raise our children to misbehave in school.*

[T]:   *Mr. Rojas, I know that by virtue of the way Felipe acts under normal circumstances. He is polite, respectful, and eager to learn. I just think in this instance he was placed in a situation where he didn't know what to do and, again, for that, I apologize.*

[P]:   *Thank you.*

[T]:   *But there is one thing that I would like your help in doing as we move forward with Felipe.*

[P]:   *Anything.*

[T]:   *Well, Felipe shared with me that he doesn't feel too good right now about the incident. He questions himself and thinks he somehow contributed to it.*

[P]:   *He told us that too.*

[T]:   *Do you think that you and Ms. Rojas could talk to Felipe again tonight about all of this and let him know that, while it was wrong to skip class, it wasn't his fault that he was being picked on? He needs to know that he is supported both at home and at school, even when he is held accountable for his actions. It's important that he know that, even though his skipping class wasn't what any of us wanted for him to do, we understand his reasoning and, more important, we know he knows what to do if he should ever find himself in that situation again—which we hope, of course, won't happen.*

[P]:   *I think we can do that.*

[T]:   *Excellent. Would you be willing to get back in touch with me tomorrow or the next day to let me know how that conversation went and how things are going for him, as far as his attitude about school is concerned? We consider parents equal partners with us in helping our kids learn to deal with both the academic and the social aspects of life. Just a phone call would be nice. And I'll get back in touch with you or Ms. Rojas later this week to let you know how things are going for Felipe here at school.*

[P]:   *That would be nice.*

[T]:   *Mr. Rojas, thanks for coming up today and working with us to make school a better place for Felipe. You are always welcome here. Please feel free to come or call anytime and, if at all possible, either you or Ms. Rojas please attend the semester parent-teacher conferences scheduled next month. Felipe is a bright young man, and I know his other teachers think highly of him and his abilities.*

What has transpired in the second half of the conference with Mr. Rojas? Ms. Sutterfield, when asked, *deferred to the parent as the authority for home discipline.* Parents will often wonder if what they do is appropriate when it comes to reinforcing school discipline. Home discipline is a family matter, unless, of course, that discipline creates a danger to the child or becomes abusive and needs to be reported. That, then, becomes our business, but in this instance, the parent's choice to ground Felipe did not seem extreme or otherwise harsh. The parent was trying to instill his own kind of accountability in his son. That, paired with the school doing the same, can be a powerful learning tool in a positive direction.

But what about the school's response to the child's infraction of skipping class? The teacher was actively involved with the principal in *applying the "geography of problem solving"* (discussed in Chapter 10) with Felipe. Ms. Sutterfield believed that it was better to work directly with Felipe in determining the type of discipline that would work best in this situation. In addition, because she believed that the misbehavior was motivated more by the child's efforts to escape maltreatment from his peers than by an actual desire to ditch class, her disciplining of Felipe *focused more on correcting the cause of the problem* than on the actual infraction itself. Rather than "bouncing" the problem to the principal and involving more "moving parts" in the application of the "discipline assembly line," Ms. Sutterfield took full responsibility for Felipe's plight. This action *demonstrated accountability* to the parent and illustrated that the teacher could be counted on to be directly involved in matters related to Felipe that involve her class.

In this conversation, Felipe was not simply a one-dimensional child. Ms. Sutterfield made several *references to the positive aspects of his behavior in the overall school environment* and did not let the one incident be the only marker of Felipe's identity discussed with the parent. Hearing that, Mr. Rojas understands that school personnel are not focused solely on misbehavior, but on the total child. This is particularly important in that it increases the likelihood that less actively involved parents will view the school as a helpful place, rather than as one where the only time they hear from school personnel is when there is a problem.

The teacher made significant efforts to *show that a working alliance was needed to increase the chances of the child's success* in dealing with this issue. Mr. Rojas was told that he was an "equal partner" in the home-school solution. The *parent was invited to share information on the progress of those home efforts* with the teacher as further evidence of the alliance. Additionally, the teacher indicated that she would follow through by making another parent contact later in the week on the progress of the child in the class. As further evidence of the teacher's and the school's efforts to involve the family in the total educational progress of Felipe, Ms. Sutterfield made it very clear that the Rojas *family was always welcome to contact the school* about any aspect of Felipe's schooling. She made special overtures to encourage one or both parents to attend the next month's parent-teacher conferences. Again, as in the dialogue with the more involved parent, every effort was made to keep the channels of communication open. With those parents whose contacts with school personnel are limited, we educators need to make *repeated invitations to work with us* as we move forward in the educator-parent alliance.

Checklists 4.1 and 4.2 summarize the main points of the approaches to both the actively involved and the less involved parent.

THE "INVERTED CURVE" AND TENSION CYCLE

One of the elements always at play when one of the conferees feels some kind of uneasiness or mistrust of the other is an increase in tension. Tension reduces our

Checklist 4.1
Encouraging Less Active Parents Whose Children Are Bullied to Join the Parent-Teacher Partnership

Respect the parent

Respond to cultural variables

Keep the discussion low-threat

Encourage the parent to ask questions

Defer to the parent as the authority in the home

Apply the geography of problem solving

Keep the focus on the issues

Demonstrate accountability through follow-up

Accentuate the positive aspects of the child's overall school experiences

Stress the importance of the parent-teacher partnership

Invite the parent to increase contacts with school personnel

Let the parent know that his or her assistance is always welcome

Checklist 4.2
Talking With Actively Involved Parents Requesting Assistance for Bullied Children

Engage the parent as a participant in the solution to the problem

Encourage the parent to understand his or her role as a team member

Practice the "3 Fs": Be firm, fair, and friendly

Be clear in responses

Be cooperative with parent concerns

Avoid defensiveness

Use preexisting positive relationships

Keep communication lines open

Avoid hidden agendas

Act in good faith

Accept accountability for oversights

Encourage the parent to continue discussions with the child at home

Stay focused/avoid distracters

Create a short-term plan to address immediate concerns

End the conference on a positive note

effectiveness in solving problems. Remember the old "inverted curve theory" (see Figure 4.1) of productivity and anxiety we all learned back in Psych 101? The greater the anxiety that exists, the less likely an individual will be to perform effectively.

When parents approach us in an unnerving manner, or if, for some reason, we just seem to be unnerved by their presence, our ability to move forward in the best problem-solving manner will be hindered. The inverted curve theory basically reminds us that when too little tension exists (such as when we get five minutes at home to plop down on the couch and surf the television with the remote), little is likely to be accomplished because the mood of relaxation tends to encourage us to stay right where we are. Under too much stress, the same occurs, but for much different reasons. Under pressure, we make more mistakes. Our "evolutionary brains" begin to take over, and we do not have the cognitive abilities to be creative. To the contrary, those old cave genes start to make us think about survival—remember fight, flight, or freeze? Obviously, fear plays a major role in how much problem-solving ability we can expend.

The optimal productivity occurs at the apex of the inverted curve. Somewhere between couch potato sloth and a fear factor frenzy lies problem-solving nirvana. We must have enough interest in what we are doing to want to do it. That "interest" we share with the concerned parent is the child's behavior. The plan becomes a vehicle that keeps that interest on a rational path toward problem solving. When we become involved in personalities or one party begins to become difficult to work with, our anxiety escalates and our productivity begins to head down the inverted curve.

Figure 4.1   The Inverted Curve of Productivity: As Stress Increases, Productivity
Decreases

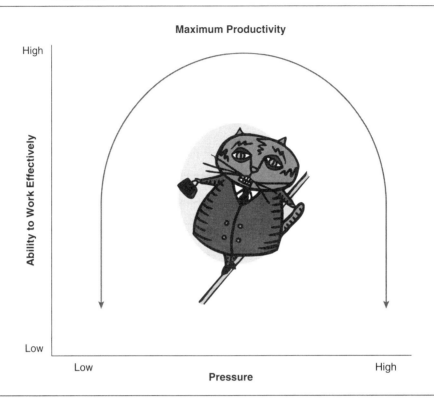

The anxiety and tension emerging during a difficult interaction tend to feed on themselves as well. Figure 4.2 visualizes the self-defeating cycle of a parent-teacher interaction using an example of the parent as the anxious individual in the conference. Truth be told, it makes little difference who is the more anxious—the cycle remains the same. We'll stay with this example of an anxious parent to illustrate what occurs during a less-than-productive parent-teacher conference.

Anxious parents who come to school probably feel the need to bring some type of "protective barrier" with them. This protective barrier may well be a defensive attitude about the reasons they are having to meet with school personnel, and that attitude may manifest itself in an attacking approach toward the teacher. Rather than taking a more moderate wait-and-see manner, the parent who attacks does so out of a strategy to maintain control of the meeting. Whether this desire to control is based on fear or intelligent design from the parent, the end result is always the same—it increases tension between the parent and the educator since the perceived attack by the parent forces the teacher to feel the need to respond defensively. The educator's response to the parent's attack creates even more tension between the two, reinforcing the parent's preconceived notion that there really is something about to occur here for which "I have to protect myself and my child." The prophecy is fulfilled. The tension escalates and spirals out of control, nothing gets done, and both parties end up feeling terrible about the interaction

Figure 4.2   The Self-Defeating Cycle of the Parent-Teacher Interaction With the Anxious Parent

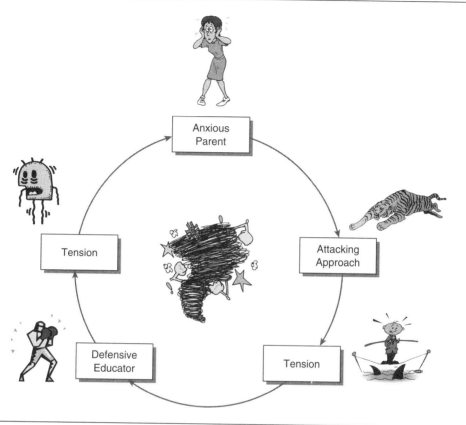

The Tension Cycle. Anxious parents who approach educators make both themselves and educators nervous, thus increasing the chances that both will miss important opportunities to develop a working alliance to solve problems of mutual interest.

and have no stomach to schedule another meeting since it will "just end up like it did the last time."

There is a way to avoid getting sucked into this self-defeating cycle. This action must occur at the point where we have that tendency to strike back when attacked by the parent. Figure 4.3 shows what happens to that self-defeating cycle when we don't respond in kind to a parent's defensive attitude.

The key to preventing the black hole of parent-teacher conference tension is to avoid responses to parent provocations that, either by design or by accident, only help throw emotional gasoline on the fire already in the room. Failing to respond in kind to parent attacks throws aggressors off their "game plans." They are not in control of the situation if they keep throwing matches into the kindling pile and nothing ignites. Our replies to their goading only throw water on the situation, not more fuel. Here are some sample neutral responses that may work to calm the provocative parent:

Figure 4.3   Breaking the Self-Defeating Cycle of the Parent-Teacher Interaction With the Anxious Parent

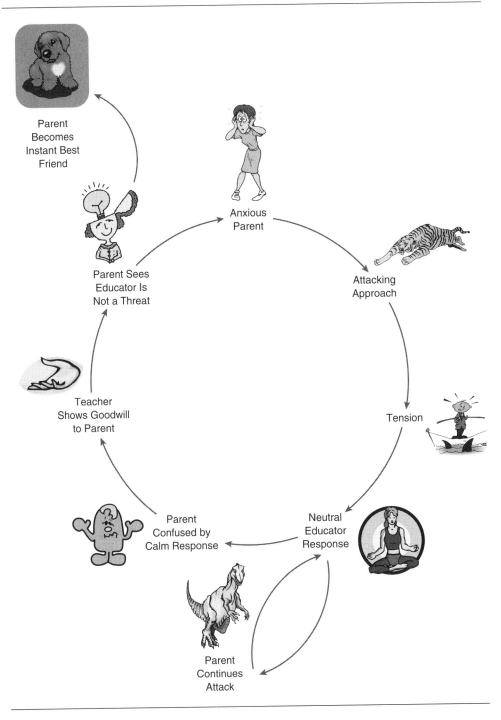

- *It's clear that you have a lot of interest in solving this problem. I can tell by your excitement that you're eager to work with us on a plan.*

- *I'm happy that you, too, are concerned about what has been happening. Your passion will go a long way toward our developing a plan to work together.*

- *I like your enthusiasm. It will be helpful as we work together on the plan that we'll be designing today.*

- *What can I do, before we get started today, to help convince you that this conference is all about moving forward and not staying focused on the past?*

The trick is to never respond directly to a harsh parent comment, unless it was so rude or offensive that it dictates a response to preserve the decorum of the conference. Anxious parents often have a lot on their minds when they get to school, and that anxiety sometimes comes out in ways that even they would prefer that it not.

The self-defeating and calm-producing conference approaches are summarized in Figures 4.2 and 4.3. Again, the key to avoiding a conference spiraling out of control is to keep the tension as manageable as possible and avoid "taking the bait" from those parents who are used to wresting control of conferences by the use of distracters. Keeping these approaches in mind will come in handy with the next group of parents that we discuss—those of children who bully others.

How to Work With Parents Whose Children Bully Others

A s difficult and awkward as it may be to work with the parents of those children who come to our attention as having been bullied, an even greater challenge awaits us when we have to address the parents of those who generate the mayhem. We may well discover, of course, very quickly from whom the intimidating child learned such behaviors! As Eron, Huesmann, and Zelli (1991) noted, there is a "rapidly accumulating body of data [suggesting] that aggression, as a characteristic way of solving interpersonal problems, usually emerges early in life. . . . [and that it] remains relatively stable across time and situation" (p. 169). But that is not always the case. So, a word of additional caution: any family can have within it an aggressive child who did not learn those behaviors from home.

SOME THINGS TO KEEP IN MIND ABOUT THE FAMILIES OF AGGRESSIVE CHILDREN

What do we know about the families of children who seem to intimidate others? Here are a few thoughts to keep in mind before we move into our first case study. Make sure to pay attention to the most important word in all of these characteristics—*may*. As Rigby (1993) points out, "the high levels of aggressiveness . . . associated with children who bully . . . may develop relatively independently of family and parental influences" (p. 511).

Studies have shown that children who are classified as bullies may come from homes in which the family members experience above-normal stress and conflict (Schwartz, Dodge, Pettit, & Bates, 1997; Smith & Myron-Wilson, 1998; Stern & Azar, 1998). These families may be more enmeshed than other families and may tend to send messages to their children that the most powerful people are the ones who get to make all the decisions (Bowers, Smith, & Binney, 1992). This dynamic can lead to an **external locus of control** that causes aggressive individuals to think that, unless acted on by a more powerful foe, their actions are acceptable. Further research has indicated that both bullies and those who were engaged in behaviors that made them both bullies and victims (classified as "bully/victims" by Bowers, Smith, & Binney [1994, p. 215]) were missing significant male role models, particularly fathers. Bully/victims were more likely to have difficulty with parental relationships and believe that their parents lacked warmth. As might be anticipated, Rigby (1993, 1994) found that the children of families with higher levels of connectedness were more likely to act prosocially and less likely to bully others, whereas adolescent bullies of both sexes were more likely to classify their families as less sympathetic, less understanding, and less well functioning.

We can use these studies—and there are many more like them—to pound home the connection between the family-of-origin and teaching-by-behavior schemas and not be wrong. But if we only assume that bullies are the products of their home and cannot be made otherwise, then we miss the plight of the parents who are bewildered by their children who developed aggressive behaviors without being exposed to them in the home. I once had an anxious mother at a workshop confront me afterward and berate me for making it seem as if all bullies are taught to behave the way they do and that it is the parents' fault for their having learned those behaviors. Never mind that that was exactly *not* what I had said and that I had emphasized the very fact that children are fully capable of absorbing poor behaviors through the **"osmosis of violence"** that permeates their lives through media and society in general. This mother knew her son had aggressive tendencies, but was hurt about the treatment she and her son were receiving from the school district and was more upset by the perception within the community that he had learned his bullying behavior in his home. Although I politely explained to her that she had not heard everything I had said, her selective hearing and personal anguish were of such a magnitude that it was clear to me that she would be unlikely to get past her frustrations. So I sacrificed myself as a whipping post until it was, mercifully, time to pack up and leave. I knew that she was truly not so upset with me personally or my message (the point of which she missed, unfortunately), but rather with her inability to get school personnel to see beyond her child's behaviors and acknowledge that she was as disappointed and frustrated about them as were the teachers and administrators.

In spite of long-standing evidence beginning with Bandura, Ross, and Ross's (1961) seminal research on imitative behaviors learned from television (the famous Bobo doll experiments), society has only begrudgingly begun to acknowledge that, well, yes, okay, we guess we'll have to admit that *maaaaaaybe* kids do imitate what they see in the media. Part of the reason for this slothlike recognition is that the media have used their resources to blow smoke in our eyes and ears, making us believe that they were not nearly as capable of influencing young lives as the evidence tended to portray. And we bought it, for the most part, until the victims of bullying began to take their own weapons to school to settle old scores with their tormentors, and we were forced to admit from the aftermath that, lo and behold, look where those kids got their ideas! Video games! Television! Internet Web sites! You mean Bandura and his crew were right, after all? Who would have ever thunk it?

TELEVISION'S IMPACT ON CHILDREN AND BULLYING

Parents have known it since shortly after the invention of television, and educators saw it in schools even before parents recognized it at home. Quite simply, "the more violence children see on television, the more likely they will think it is a normal, acceptable part of life" (Perlmutter, 1994). In one of the most stark examples of television's impact on children, after the introduction of television in a remote section of Canada in the 1970s, young elementary-aged children's aggressive behaviors and physical assaults increased 160 percent (Centerwall, 1992; Williams, 1986). And the growing levels of access that even young children have to violent media images—the Kaiser Family Foundation (2003, 2005) has reported that 36% of children younger than age 6 have televisions in their rooms, 39% use a computer several times or more a week, and 65% live in households where the television set is on more often than not—increase the likelihood that children will continue to "learn their attitudes about violence at a very early age" since those attitudes "tend to last" (American Academy of Pediatrics, n.d.). With estimates that children watch between 23 and 28 hours of television each week and that, in doing so, they are exposed to 200,000 acts of virtual violence (of which 40,000 portray murder) by the age of 18 (Hurst, 2004); that, by the late 1990s, over 60% of programming contained some element of violence (U.S. Office of the Surgeon General, 2001); and that the latest neurological data show that violence-themed video games have a direct impact on the emotional arousal area of the brain (Morley, 2006; Reinberg, 2006), is it any wonder that educators are likely to have to discuss bullying behaviors with the parents of children who mimic what they see on a daily basis?

Case Study: Parent of an Aggressive Child

Jenny Pepper is a sixth-grade girl who has been reported a number of times to her teachers as badgering other girls. Jenny is very bright. A lot of her activities have gone on "under the radar" and unnoticed by teachers, yet her targets have complained about them. She has been accused of spreading rumors throughout the school about peers she does not like. She has repeatedly been mentioned as the person responsible for pasting nasty computer-generated notes in the girls' bathrooms about those same individuals. Because Jenny is so quick-witted, she has been able to avoid detection until just recently. As a result of three teachers "connecting the dots" between mischievous events over the past three weeks, she has finally been confirmed as the ringleader of a malicious effort to defame one target in particular: Malika. Ms. Wilson, Jenny's primary sixth-grade teacher, has called for a conference with Mrs. Pepper.

Teacher [T]: *Thanks for coming in to see me today, Mrs. Pepper.*

Parent [P]: *Well, I'm here, but I really don't see what the problem is. Jenny told me what you wanted to see me about and I don't see why it's such a big deal. This is normal kid behavior.*

[T]: *What exactly did Jenny explain to you about all of this?*

[P]:   *She told me that you teachers have accused her of picking on several of her friends, but that she's only done it a few times and only because of that one girl—what's her name?—Malika, that's it—because that Malika girl has been stirring up trouble with Jenny's friends and trying to turn them against her. It's pretty clear to me that Jenny's just defending herself.*

Let's stop just 30 seconds into this case study to identify the presumptions that this parent is bringing with her to the conference.

It is clear that Mrs. Pepper is not happy about being asked to come to school to address her daughter's misbehavior. Her defensiveness is evident from the first words out of her mouth. Additionally, the parent believes that her daughter is not to blame for whatever she has done. She views Jenny's behaviors as a response to intimidation from others. Mrs. Pepper's response could be warranted, provided that Jenny's recounting of the situation left out several of the important details regarding her own involvement in the mayhem, which it likely did.

The teacher, to this point, *does not respond to the verbal skepticism of the parent.* She has simply asked a clarification question to determine exactly what it is that the parent thinks she understands about the need for a conference.

[T]:   *Mrs. Pepper, we'll get into all of the details of what we know about Jenny's behaviors as we move forward. I want to tell you at the outset that the purpose of our meeting today is to ask your help in working with all of us to make Jenny's time here at school the most educational it can be. It's not about punishment, but about holding Jenny accountable for her actions when she makes a mistake, as well as to keep our school a safe place to learn.*

[P]:   *But she didn't do anything except give back what she got from that Malika girl.*

[T]:   *Well, let me share with you what we have observed here about Jenny's behaviors with her peers over the past few weeks and you can compare that with what she has shared with you, okay?*

[P]:   *I'm sure it's the same things she told me.*

[T]:   *Well, hopefully. Let's see. . . .*

The *teacher stays focused on the purpose of the conference* in spite of the parent's continued provocations and intimations that the teacher is wrong. Parents of aggressive children may tend to resist evidence about their children's behaviors, especially if they support those behaviors as a sign of strength or, as the research made clear in the first part of the chapter, if the parents use such behaviors in their homes to resolve their own family dilemmas. Ms. Wilson also states, as soon as she can considering the resistance of the parent to listen, what the purpose of the conference is—not punishment, but to ensure accountability and an increase in the likelihood of improving the learning environment. Mrs. Pepper is attempting to throw her own distracters at the teacher in an effort to safeguard Jenny from blame. As the teacher focuses on the larger purpose—improving education for all children—the parent may feel less of a need to defend her child's misbehavior since improving education for all children includes her own as well.

A major portion of the conference takes place outside the venue of this script. In that part of the conference, Ms. Wilson *provides factual evidence* to the parent of specific behaviors that Jenny has participated in over the past three weeks. *Providing factual behavioral evidence is absolutely essential in keeping both the parent and the teacher focused on the mission of the conference.* The conference is not about "bashing" the child (no matter how difficult or challenging the child's behaviors may be), nor is it about making the parent feel like she is a "bad parent." Conferences with parents of children who bully must not get sidetracked by personality clashes or by matters over which the teacher has no control, namely, the parenting skills of the parent. As the old saying goes, facts are stubborn little things. They make it difficult to argue to the contrary.

Ms. Wilson provides Mrs. Pepper with a list of behavioral infractions committed by Jenny and directed against her peers over the last three weeks. The list is *presented in a low-threat manner* and in a matter-of-fact mode. After all, that's exactly what the list includes—observational facts that the faculty has accumulated since they figured out that Jenny was creating problems for her peers. At the conclusion of the review of the incidents, the conference continues as follows:

[T]:   *I know that's quite a list of behaviors that we have observed with Jenny over the past three weeks. How does this square with what she explained to you?*

[P]:   *Well, she didn't mention all of those things, but then I wouldn't expect her to since she knows that I know that she wasn't responsible for all the things that she did. Like I said, she was only responding to the things that that Malika girl was doing to her.*

[T]:   *Regardless of what she may have shared with you, Mrs. Pepper, we have quite a bit of behavior here that we need to discuss—*

[P]:   *What are you going to do with the other girls?*

[T]:   *We have dealt with all of the other girls as we believed best under the circumstances.*

[P]:   *What did you do to them?*

[T]:   *We are not allowed to discuss other students with parents unless we have those parents' permission, I'm sorry. I also have to point out, Mrs. Pepper, that, as far as we can tell, Jenny was responsible for everything that has occurred over the past few weeks—the incidents in the lunchroom, the taping of the nasty posters in the bathrooms, the passing of the notes which I shared with you, and the pushing and shoving during band class. And it's not just what I have watched Jenny do to her friends; please remember that two other teachers have witnessed these things too.*

[P]:   *Well, I still don't think that Jenny should be punished for what she's not responsible for.*

[T]:   *Mrs. Pepper, believe me, we don't want to punish Jenny. We want her to learn from this experience that she cannot behave in this manner here at school and that, if she does, she will be held accountable for her behaviors. And we would like your help, as well, in helping her make the changes we need her to make as we move forward.*

[P]:   *So, what do you think I can do?*

[T]:   *Actually, Mrs. Pepper, there's a lot you can help us with and I hope that you will.*

At this point, the **leverage** of the conference has begun to move forward. Leveraging refers to critical moments during a problem-solving dialogue when one party or the other gains some sort of "toehold" and can move the conversation forward toward achieving a goal. Notice, I say "a" goal, not "the" goal, since each party in the room may have a different one. Mrs. Pepper's goal is to keep the focus off of Jenny and make the situation appear to be less her fault than that of her peers. Ms. Wilson's goal is to try to move Mrs. Pepper toward an alliance in helping correct Jenny's misbehaviors. Leveraging works best when both parties agree to move toward a mutual goal, but as this scenario illustrates, that is not always the case. Therefore, it helps when the educator is able to *recognize leveraging moments* during a parent-teacher conference. Such moments occur when there is a forward motion in the direction of the goal. In this instance, the leveraging moment came when Mrs. Pepper asked what she might be able to do to solve the problem, instead of offering another excuse for her daughter's behavior. It is critical to jump at the chance when it occurs and get that toehold before the less motivated party slips back into a noncooperative response pattern. When the opportunity presents itself, take it!

[T]:   *Mrs. Pepper, we believe that the best way to solve problems with children is when both the school and the parents work together. Personally, I don't think we do enough of that, which is all the more reason why I think that this conference with you today is important.*

[P]:   *I'm not convinced it's that important.*

[T]:   *Well, if we can leave today agreeing that both of us have a stake in Jennifer's well-being and that we both can be a part of the solution to the problem we're talking about right now, that will be a big step in moving toward making things better.*

[P]:   *Okay, so, what do you have in mind?*

Slowly the teacher *continues to leverage the conversation in a positive direction* and away from the parent's original refusal to entertain any notion about trying to resolve the situation. The *teacher maintains steady leveraging pressure* toward the direction that is thought to increase the likelihood of bringing the parent around to considering becoming a part of the problem-solving alliance. The conference is at an even more critical point now as the teacher has managed to get the parent interested or at least to ask a question about exactly what her role might be in helping from the home front.

[T]:   *Specifically, we believe that it will be helpful if you reinforce at home the message that we have given to Jenny here at school that it is not acceptable to behave in the way that she has been doing over the last few weeks.*

[P]:   *But I've told you a thousand times that it's not her fault!*

[T]:   *We'll just have to disagree on that point, Mrs. Pepper, but please hear me out and then we'll go back over everything to review any concerns that you have.*

The teacher continues to keep that slow and steady pressure on the parent to *leverage the conversation toward the plan* that the school believes is essential for the parent to participate in, even though the parent remains skeptical. At the same time, the teacher is *making an attempt to move away from the parent's insistence that the child is not at fault.* This may or may not work, as we will see in the next chapter when things go astray. However, in this instance, Ms. Wilson is convincing in a "friendly sort of way" and is able to keep the parent interested enough to listen. The teacher continues with the plan:

[T]:   *Specifically, here's how we need your help. First, like I said, it will be helpful if you can reinforce the message at home that it is not acceptable to behave in the way Jenny has been behaving over the past few weeks. She needs to understand that the school is a place where we come to learn and that everyone can't learn to the best of their abilities unless they are treated with respect—and that includes Jenny. We make certain that Jenny is not mistreated here at school by her peers. I know we disagree on that point based on what she has told you, but we—*

[P]:   *Are you saying that Jenny's a liar?*

[T]:   *No, I'm saying that we have not observed the behaviors directed toward her from her peers that she has told you that she has received. Quite honestly, we know that things go on among kids that we don't see, but based on our evidence of the past three weeks we have seen nothing to support what she has shared with you. Please let me move on and then I'll be more than happy to answer all your questions.*

[P]:   [Parent says nothing, but also does not interject anything, either.]

[T]:   *We want Jenny to know that school is a safe place for everyone, including her, and that she plays a role in helping it be that way for everyone else too. Second, we need your help in letting Jenny know that if she continues to behave the same way that she has been that she will continue to be held accountable for her actions. That means that we at school will expect her to follow the rules and make amends to whomever she has hurt, regardless if that hurt has come by either words or deeds. Third, it would be helpful if Jenny hears from you that she can also share with us any problems she might be having with her friends, just like you say that she has been sharing with you now. She needs to understand that both of us are working together—you at home and we here at school—and that we are comparing notes, so to speak. Which really is my last point. Jenny needs to understand that we are a team working together and that we are not bashful about meeting when we need to discuss her behaviors or any problems that she might be experiencing. We don't want her to think that we at school don't care what happens to her just because of this incident, that we think that she is a "bad egg." We care about her in more ways than just this one particular matter.*

> *I have these four points listed on a sheet of paper for you to consider, and I'd like to give you the chance to ask me anything about any of this, especially if you think there's something here that you don't feel comfortable with or that you feel can't be done.*

Wow! This was an extremely critical moment in the parent-teacher conference. Look at all that transpired. The *focus was shifted entirely onto the explanation of a plan*, something that the parent could do at home. The *plan was specific*. It was *short* and relatively *simple*. Basically, all the parent is being asked to do is to reinforce the school expectations of student behavior. The plan was even provided to the parent in a *written format* to *give the parent a chance to review it and ask questions or make comments*, which is exactly what must occur in the next step: The *parent must be given the chance to respond* to the proposal and, with reasonable modifications as necessary, be given the chance to "buy into" it to increase his or her sense of "ownership." **Ownership of a plan** increases the likelihood of following it and one's level of **commitment** to it. Particularly if a parent is given a role to play in the alliance, it helps if he or she truly feels as if he or she has participated in its design (in this case, through either acceptance or modification of the proposal).

Now the control of what happens next has been returned to the parent. In essence, the teacher has given leverage back to the parent to do what she may with the proposed plan. In the worst of cases, the parent could attack it and reject it. In that perfect world where we'd all like to live, Mrs. Pepper would joyously thank Ms. Wilson for designing such a perfect plan and would dance out of the room on her way to new levels of parental bliss at the newfound understanding of her partnership in the teacher-parent alliance. That usually doesn't happen, of course. What is more likely to occur is something like this:

[P]:   [Looks at the sheet of paper with the four-part plan.] *I'm still not convinced that we need to do anything at home to help out. These silly four little things— that's what they are, silly, you know—we can do them at the house, but I can't guarantee that they'll work.*

[T]:   *All we're asking, Mrs. Pepper, is that you'll give them a try and let us know how they work. Is there anything on that list that you think that you cannot do or that needs to be modified in any way?*

[P]:   *I'm not sure that I can convince her that you people up here are not out to get her. That's that last point on the list. We both wonder if maybe all this stuff isn't just about the opposite, that you people are out to get her and ignore all the stuff that that Malika girl and her friends have been doing to Jenny. I mean, I can do all the stuff on this list, but Jenny's a smart girl and she'll probably just laugh at everything I say.*

[T]:   *Hopefully not, especially if you can convince her that what we're talking about is a serious matter. But is there anything specific on the list that you see as troublesome or that you really, truly believe can't be done?*

[P]:   *Well, again, I just think the whole thing is a waste of my time—and Jenny's. But if it will make you happy, I'll do it.*

[T]:　*Mrs. Pepper, I really don't want you to do anything that you don't think will work with Jenny or that you don't believe is in her best interest. So, if you don't believe that any of this will work, then let's try and decide on some other things together that we believe will work. I'm open to suggestions and I'm really trying hard to make things better for everyone concerned.*

What has the teacher done? First, she *allowed the parent to voice her opinions* about the proposal. That opinion was not a positive one, but it was not an altogether outright condemnation either. Low-level criticism of a plan from a critical or skeptical parent may well indicate more acceptance than rejection. Nothing that Mrs. Pepper said was a direct response to the proposal so much as it was the expression of displeasure toward the entire school for its holding Jenny accountable for her actions. This was another attempt by the parent to throw the focus back on a distracter issue, but even then, it was a rather halfhearted effort. *The teacher stayed focused on the plan* and *made repeated efforts to encourage the parent to amend it* as she thought best. At *no point was the teacher defensive.* If anything, the *teacher was on the offense to try to get the parent to offer any suggestion* to make the plan better. This is just one more way to keep the doors of communication open between parents and teachers while discussing difficult issues about a child. If parents choose to shut those doors, that is their choice, but educators do not want to be the ones who first make that move unless extenuating circumstances exist, such as the emergence of hostility from a parent to the point that an educator feels unsafe. In those instances, self-preservation demands showing hostile parties the door out of the building!

[P]:　*Okay. I can do this with Jenny, but I can't guarantee you any results. You people up here have to do your jobs better too.*

[T]:　*Mrs. Pepper, I assure you that we are constantly trying to do that. But we also know that the more help we get from home, the more heads we get together working with our kids both in school and in the home, the greater the likelihood that something good will occur for everyone. All we would like you to do is try these things and let us know how they work. We'll do our part here at school to keep you informed on what we see happening with Jenny, and I'd like to be able to call you later this week to chat about how all of this is working, both at school and Jenny's reactions at home. Could we give this a try and, if it doesn't work, meet again to try to design something else?*

[P]:　*Well, this better work because I don't intend to have to come up here all the time talking about all this silly kid stuff. I have work to do, you know.*

[T]:　*As long as you know that you can always contact us about any aspect of Jenny's education. We're here to help, and we need your help too.*

The *conference ends on a positive note* and with the doors of communication remaining open—at least from the teacher's standpoint. Although the parent is not completely accepting of every aspect of the conference, she at least understands that the school is making every effort possible to make a currently unacceptable situation better for everyone in the long run.

KISSING A PLAN INCREASES THE CHANCES OF SUCCESS FOR EVERYONE

In this case study, a skeptical parent was leveraged into finally accepting a role in the problem-solving alliance. Key to this success is presenting a plan that follows the basic rules of Planning 101: *K*eep *I*t *S*hort and *S*imple. We educators tend to babble in eduspeak most of the time, but such language is intimidating to parents and provides just one more reason for them to stay away from us! Short and simple language in plans helps offset a parent's uneasiness about buying into any such problem-solving approach that includes them in the mix.

The best KISSed plans are those that are also *doable* and *achievable* at some levels. Ms. Wilson's plan that she presented to Mrs. Pepper had only four points. If there had been fewer, so much the better. We do not want to overwhelm the parent with a tremendous amount of things to do. After all, we want them to help us; we don't want to scare them away with a 200-point plan to solve global warming, reduce world hunger, create world peace, and, oh yes, by the way, this will help your child stop being a bully too.

To make a plan doable, we have to take into account the ability of the parents to actively do what we are asking them to do. We have to make professional decisions from (sometimes) limited information as to the kind of parent support we are likely to obtain from the home. Is this parent willing to try to work with the child to employ our suggestions? Is the parent-child relationship such that the child is likely to respond to a parent's overture? Is the parent capable of implementing a proposed plan? The answers to these questions are likely to be discovered during the review and commitment stages of the parent-teacher conference as discussed above.

Do not equate achievable with completely solving the problem from home. Plans that are achievable in the long run have many smaller achievable steps built in to ensure steady progress toward the overall mission. The biggest mistake that we make in planning with parents as partners is that we forget that getting from one end of the field to the other is achieved most often through a long series of possessions of the ball, rather than one big "touchdown play." Mrs. Pepper is far more likely to keep plugging away at the proposed plan—a plan, remember, that she is not too wild about in the first place—if she observes some true progress as she makes efforts to do what she was asked to do. If we give a reluctant parent a task that is too difficult or likely to fail at the outset, it reaffirms the belief that it was "too hard" or "stupid" or "I told them it wouldn't work." Therefore, it is essential that we *build in as many* **automatic successes** *as possible* to help the parent be motivated to continue to work with the child.

In the case study with Mrs. Pepper, what are the automatic successes built into the plan offered by Ms. Wilson? The very first one is just the request to relay a message to Jenny from the teacher that school is supposed to be a safe place for everyone, including her, and that she plays a role in helping create that safe place. What does that involve? Not much, just the willingness of the parent to relay the message. True, it helps if the parent actually believes what she is saying and is not just mouthing the words with little conviction, but having the parent to do something as simple as *reinforce a message at home* is a relatively easy thing to do.

The second part of the plan is little different from the first part. Mrs. Pepper is to emphasize a second message to Jenny—that she will be held accountable if she continues to misbehave. The importance of reinforcing the school's message at home cannot be overemphasized. If children have been receiving active or tacit approval of their misbehavior from their parents, then they believe that the whole family endorses that behavior. In essence, the child believes that "Mom and Dad are right, the school is wrong." If suddenly the parents "switch sides" and ally themselves with school personnel, the child receives a powerful message that such misbehavior is less likely to be endorsed *anywhere*, either at school or at home, and that the likelihood of finding a sympathetic adult ear condoning such has quickly vanished. Likewise, this change in support from the parents to a partnership with the teacher may also create confusion in the child's future planned mayhem: "If Mom and Dad are not going to believe everything I tell them and back those teachers next time I put gum in Malika's hair, maybe I'd better lay low and come up with a different game plan just to see how serious they really are about this change-a-roo stuff." Of course, ultimately, the parents are going to have to follow through with their newly announced expectations, so part of the immediate change for the positive in a child's behavior may well be predicated on the child's efforts to test the parents' willingness to actually do what they said they would.

The third and fourth parts of the plan with Mrs. Pepper are no more risky for the parent than the first two. Both of these parts let the child know that, even though the rules have changed, that doesn't mean that the child doesn't still have a loving parent at home who wants to hear about the experiences of the day. That door of communication is still open and, more important (though it is not likely that Jenny will care about it on first hearing of the new plan), not only does the parent continue to care about what happens in school, but so do her teachers. If Jenny has been acting out from some kind of misperception that the adults in her life don't care about her (which is sometimes the convoluted message kids get when their parents ignore them and then criticize the personnel who are forced to intervene at school when the child acts in ways intended to garner attention), this part of the plan is designed to offset that belief system.

In summary, this is a very KISSed plan with lots of built-in automatic successes for the parent if the parent will only take the initiative. All the parent has been asked to do, in the case study above, is to talk with the child about reinforcing the behavioral expectations of the school. The one thing that the parent may find most difficult to do, as is often the case with less cooperative and skeptical parents, is avoid being as negative toward those school rules in the future. Although, on the surface, that may seem to be a major change for the parent (and, for a few, it may well be!), we will never know unless we make the effort to provide the parent with different tools to work with us than they have been using in the past. Plan 5.1, located at the end of this chapter, offers a sample KISSed plan that can be used with parents like Mrs. Pepper. In this scenario, the plan was a typed copy of the plan worked out by Ms. Wilson and Mrs. Pepper and e-mailed to Mrs. Pepper the evening of the conference.

Below is a summary list of the main points discussed in this chapter on ways to approach the reluctant parent:

- Stay focused on the issue.
- Do not respond to parent skepticism.
- Use low-threat approaches with the parent.
- Provide facts about the child's behavior.
- Recognize leveraging moments.
- Leverage the parent toward developing a plan.
- Let the parent respond and provide input to the plan.
- Obtain parent commitment to the plan.
- End on a positive note.

Plan 5.1   Proposed Behavior Plan for Jenny Pepper

Date 10.14.07

Who Designed This Plan?

Ms. Wilson met with Mrs. Pepper on 10.14.07 to discuss Jenny's recent behaviors. Mrs. Pepper and Ms. Wilson both agreed to the following plan to help correct Jenny's behaviors and help increase positive peer relationships.

What Are Our Goals?

Immediate: Reduce Jenny's instances of negative behavior toward peers.
Long-term: Improve Jenny's relationships with her friends.

What Specific Behaviors Are We Targeting?

1. Stop (immediately) Jenny's pushing and shoving of peers while on school property.

2. Stop (immediately) Jenny's use of improper language and name calling directed toward peers.

3. Help Jenny reduce (early) and then stop (entirely) the passing of notes with demeaning comments about peers.

4. Improve Jenny's attitude toward school in general.

What Will School Personnel Do?

1. Teachers who have Jenny in classes will meet to discuss Jenny's recent behaviors prior to contacting parents for conference. ACCOMPLISHED 10.12.07

2. Lead teacher (Ms. Wilson) will schedule and meet with one or both of Jenny's parents. PARENT CONTACTED 10.13.07/MEETING HELD 10.14.07 WITH MRS. PEPPER WHO WILL BE THE CONTACT PARENT IN THE HOME.

3. Lead teacher and Mrs. Pepper will meet and design plan to improve Jenny's behavior. ACCOMPLISHED 10.14.07

4. Ms. Wilson will update all teachers who have Jenny in class as to the proposed plan and assign specific teacher assignments on how best to resolve the behaviors. SCHEDULED FOR 10.15.07

How Can the Parent Help?

1. Mrs. Pepper will discuss with Jenny that school is supposed to be a safe place for everyone, including her. SCHEDULED FOR 10.15-16.07)

2. Mrs. Pepper will discuss with Jenny that she will be held responsible for her negative behaviors toward her friends if they continue in the future. SCHEDULED FOR 10.15-16.07

3. Mrs. Pepper will let Jenny know that if she has any problems related to her friends, she can share that information both at home and with teachers at school. SCHEDULED FOR 10.15-16.07

4. Mrs. Pepper will stress with Jenny that both teachers at school and her parents are working together to try to help Jenny improve her behaviors. SCHEDULED FOR 10.15-16.07

What Will Jenny Do?

1. Jenny will meet with Ms. Wilson about the plan on the day after the discussion with Ms. Wilson. SCHEDULED FOR EITHER 10.16 or 17.07

2. Jenny will start working on improving her behaviors immediately after parent-teacher conference. NOTE: JENNY BEGAN TO SHOW IMPROVEMENT REGARDING SOME OF THE TARGET BEHAVIORS ON THE DAY AFTER THE CONFERENCE WAS SCHEDULED.

How Will We Follow Up With Each Other?

1. Mrs. Pepper will call Ms. Wilson on the day after the home conversation to provide information as to how Jenny reacted to the discussion. SCHEDULED FOR EITHER 10.16 or 17.07

2. Ms. Wilson will contact Mrs. Pepper by phone at the end of the week to update her on Jenny's progress for the week. SCHEDULED FOR 10.18.07

3. Ms. Wilson will meet with Jenny's other teachers to discuss her behaviors in the next week following the parent-teacher conference. SCHEDULED FOR NO LATER THAN 10.23.07

4. Ms. Wilson will contact the parents by phone to update them on Jenny's progress at the end of the week after the conference. SCHEDULED FOR NO LATER THAN 10.25.07

5. If another meeting is needed, Mrs. Pepper can contact Ms. Wilson at any time to schedule an appointment.

Cc: Principal via email

Mrs. Pepper via email and hard copy

Student file

CHAPTER SIX

The Parent Who
Refuses to Cooperate

Undoubtedly, some of the most vexing interactions we have in school are the ones are with parents who refuse to cooperate when their child is responsible for bullying others. Unlike those in the case studies we have previously reviewed, these parents often fit the stereotypical pattern mythologized in teachers' lounges. They are role models for their children's behaviors. They view the school as the enemy, and the educator is never right. For whatever reason, these parents are not willing to entertain the vaguest notions of cooperating with school personnel, yet we must somehow continue to work with them for the sake of their misbehaving child. It is not a pleasant set of expectations from which to start, and the outcome is often bleak.

SUBVERTING THE DOMINANT PARADIGM

We've all heard the expression, "subverting the dominant paradigm," but perhaps we have never considered it as one of the most powerful tools for working with difficult situations and people. Too often in education we keep doing the same things over and over while expecting different results. Albert Einstein offered this as his own definition of insanity: doing the same thing over and over again and expecting different results! It's true that practice makes perfect, and there is nothing better than experience in the classroom to teach us how to actually do all the things we were taught to do in the education classes we took for our degrees. However, at some point perhaps we need to hear Einstein's voice in the back of our heads and think about how what he was saying applies to what we are doing about problems that don't get any better.

Like their children, the parents of children who bully do not engender a lot of goodwill from us or inspire a willingness on our parts to want to work with them. They punch *our* buttons, and they may well engage in bullying behaviors toward school personnel during our efforts to engage them in constructive dialogue. Who wants to help someone who doesn't want our help, who thinks we're only after their kids to get them in trouble, and who, on top of everything else, is nasty in their own behaviors toward us? Not most teachers and, in truth, me neither! McEwan (2005) refers to these parents as "angry, troubled . . . or just plan crazy" (p. xvi).

But what if we did something entirely different with those parents to "throw them off their game"? Parents who are the most difficult are used to controlling the situation. They know how to leverage a conversation *their* way because they know what *we* typically do. That's right, they know what we are going to do because they've had lots of experience frustrating and confusing us in our efforts to work with them. So, what if we didn't do that? What if we, instead, refused to do what they expected us to do? What if we subverted the parents' dominant paradigm by refusing to respond to all the old tricks that they have used with educators—and most likely other people too—for all these years?

Hmmmm. I wonder what would happen? I feel another case study coming on.

Case Study of the Parent Who Refuses to Cooperate

Paul Leny is an eighth grader who has been identified by every teacher in the school as aggressive. He pushes and shoves his peers during class changes. He is often angry and sullen and, of late, has taken to harassing those seventh graders who are smaller than he is. When approached by teachers and instructed to correct his behaviors, he acts as if he has done nothing wrong and complains that the teachers are just picking on him because he is the one who happened to get caught. Paul's family has been notified on at least two occasions about his behavior—once by letter, the second time by phone. After an incident in the cafeteria, the principal was going to suspend him until Paul's homeroom teacher, Mr. Hatch, asked for a chance to intervene on his behalf. Mr. Hatch has asked for the chance to leverage a meeting with one or both of Paul's parents in an effort to engage them in a working alliance to reduce his mistreatment of his peers and thereby avoid the principal's suspension.

The first contact between Mr. Hatch and Paul's home is by phone. Paul's mother agrees to pass a message along to his father, Paul Sr., to come to school tomorrow since "Paul Sr. handles all the discipline around the house." Mr. Leny does, indeed, show up the next day as planned, immediately after the end of the last class of the day.

Mr. Hatch [T]:	*Mr. Leny, thank you for coming today. I really am glad to meet you and look forward to working with you to help with Paul's school experience.*
Mr. Leny [P]:	[Shakes hands and sits down.] *Well, I'm not glad to be here, if the truth is told. I had to take off work early, and I can't see why you people can't just solve these problems yourselves.*
[T]:	*It may seem easy on the surface, Mr. Leny, but we need your help in solving some behaviors of Paul's that have been creating several problems for him and other students.*
[P]:	*He's told me about several of the incidents that have gone on. That stuff's just kid stuff. He didn't hurt anyone in any of them. Don't you people know how to handle kids?*

[T]:   *We learn more about that very subject every day, I assure you. Kids always come up with something new, don't they?*

[P]:   *Not really, as far as I can tell. It's always been that way, so what's different about it now?*

Several things are clear at this juncture. From his very first exchanges, Mr. Leny seems not to be willing to be very cooperative. It is *important that the teacher not overreact* to these first interactions and impressions. The parent may feel uncomfortable in the situation, and his awkwardness may be revealed in less-than-delicate phrasing. Mr. Hatch is making every effort to *accommodate the parent's opinions* (provocations?) up to this point and *avoid a stumbling block during the first minutes* of the conference.

[T]:   *Actually, there is a difference in the way these things are viewed and dealt with today. When you and I were growing up, adults seemed to overlook a lot of the kinds of behavior that Paul's been involved in lately and we got the message that it was all "kid stuff," like you said. But we know now that some of that "kid stuff" was then, and is now, really hurtful to kids and prevents them from learning as much as they should in school. I'd like to review with you everything that has happened up to this point with Paul and what the school's position is. May I?*

[P]:   *You can do what you like; that's what I'm up here for, right? But I think all of this fuss is a load of crap and that it's just another sign of how sissified things are in schools today.*

[T]:   [Ignores Mr. Leny's comments and moves directly to the list of behavioral problems that Paul has recently exhibited. Mr. Leny listens during the review, but says nothing.] *So, you see, Paul's behaviors are not just little things. They have involved a lot of physical pushing and shoving, verbal abuse, and then that incident in the cafeteria when he poured the milk down the girl's shirt was just too much for everyone involved.*

[P]:   *So? What's the big deal?*

[T]:   *Is there anything about any of these incidents that you would like to share with me from things that Paul has discussed with you that would give me some insight as to why he does them?*

[P]:   *We don't talk about that stuff. They're all no big deal, anyway, like I said. He's just a boy with a lot of energy who's practicing what we've told him at home. You don't take crap from people, and sometimes people need to be reminded just who they are.*

[T]:   *What exactly does that mean, "who they are"?*

[P]:   *Just that some people think that they're better than others and that a little reminder every now and then puts them back in their place.*

[T]:   *Mr. Leny, we can't overlook Paul's pouring milk down the back of a girl's shirt in the cafeteria and embarrassing her in front of all her peers. Would you agree that that is something that is unacceptable behavior for one kid to do to another?*

[P]:   *Maybe. Depends on if she deserved it or not. Some of those seventh-grade girls can be awfully snotty, you know.*

Here is more evidence of how difficult the conference is likely to be. The parent continues to counter virtually every one of the teacher's observations by downplaying its significance or by attempting to use a distracter to focus the attention away from Paul's misdeeds. The *teacher repeatedly ignores the challenges* and *stays focused on the primary topic, the behavior* of the child. Mr. Hatch even makes an effort to inquire about any information that the parent might have from home that would shed a different light on Paul's behaviors, only to be rebuffed by more justification of those behaviors by the parent. Unfortunately, in this instance, the first impression the teacher had of the parent was accurate and a harbinger of what is to come—more of the same. However, the *teacher refuses to become flustered by the parent's distracters* and presses on:

[T]:   *Let me focus on my main concern today, Mr. Leny, and I'll just be very clear and frank. The principal is going to suspend Paul for three days over the milk incident unless you and I can work out something better for Paul.*

[P]:   *What! Three days for that? He must really be a dumbass if he thinks that a little milk is worth a three-day suspension.*

[T]:   *Actually, the principal is a she, and I think it best if we both keep our comments as civil as possible, okay? I wouldn't want anyone to get the wrong impression from our conference.*

[P]:   *I don't care what anyone thinks!*

[T]:   *Well, I think we both care about Paul or we wouldn't be here now—*

[P]:   *The only reason I'm here is because you people are just nuts about some little something that happened that is no big deal and now you're going to kick Paul out for nothing,*

[T]:   *Mr. Leny, I'm trying the best I can to prevent just that. If you'll just give me another minute or two, I think you'll be happier over what I'm going to propose instead of a suspension from the principal.*

[P]:   *I didn't come up here happy and I'm not going to leave here happy, so you can try and "happy" me all you want, but it's not going to change things as far as I'm concerned.*

[T]:   *Will you let me offer those suggestions, anyway, just to see if you find any of them worth pursuing?*

[P]:   *No, I really don't want to hear them. You people just want to kick my son out. Go ahead. See if I care. But when he comes back, nothing's going to change. He's still going to be the same kid and we're still going to back him like we do now.*

[T]:   *I really wish you'd give me a chance with what I'd like to propose.*

[P]:   *No, keep your proposals. I'm outta' here.*

[T]:   *Before you go, Mr. Leny, please know that if you ever would like to talk to anyone about Paul's school progress, I would be more than willing to do so with you or Mrs. Leny. Please know that.*

[P]:   *Yeah, whatever.* [Exits the room.]

Was the teacher to blame for the parent's attitude and behavior? No. In this instance, it was Mr. Hatch who was trying to prevent the child from being suspended by offering an alternative to the principal's suspension, if only the parent would agree to it. The *teacher constantly refused to "take the bait" of the parent's efforts to leverage the conference* (remember Figure 4.3 on breaking the tension cycle?) in the way with which he was most familiar—toward the distracters of how Paul's behaviors were the result of others' annoyances and the school's failure to minimize his infractions. Mr. Hatch continually tried to keep the focus on avoiding the suspension and getting Mr. Leny to hear the alternative plan. It wasn't anything the teacher said that ended the conference before the goal was accomplished. That decision was made by the parent, who ended any hope for Mr. Hatch's plan to bear fruit when he left the room. In doing so, the parent maintained control of the conference, much like he controls most other conversations in his life—it's his way or no way.

CONFLICT RESOLUTION WITH PARENTS WHO REFUSE TO COOPERATE

When the parent refuses to engage in the process of compromise, we are not responsible for the failure of interventions on behalf of children. Likewise, we have to be certain that we educators are not the ones who fail to recognize the need to compromise during the difficult task of working with parents who are uncooperative. It is often difficult to give up the ownership of plans that we have designed on behalf of a child, and it is easy to react defensively when those plans are outright rejected or ignored by parents who seem to have little concern for the problem we are trying to work with them to solve. What an insult! However, we also have to remember that the job of the professional is to *offer* advice and counsel to parents; we cannot make them *take* that advice. Like medical doctors who repeatedly advise their patients to quit smoking and lose weight—and then those patients don't—our jobs are to offer the recommendations, not do the work for the parents.

Conflict resolution is predicated on the premise that two parties in dispute can come to some kind of solution if the proper conditions for change are present. Both sides must be willing to agree to alter their original positions—the differences between them are usually the crux of the problem in the first place. Ideally, when both sides are willing to alter their original positions, both sides end up "getting something" from the interaction. Drew (2002) has referred to this as a "win-win" situation. Although neither side gets everything it wanted, both sides end up with a part of a principle that they feel is important to them under the conditions of disagreement. In the end, half a loaf is better than no loaf at all.

There are many different avenues toward conflict resolution. Different groups may use different approaches, and the approaches used in the workplace for employees may be different from the approaches used with parents and children in the schools. However, all approaches provide potential avenues of solution when working with parents who are considered to be uncooperative. Below are 11 global concepts underlying conflict resolution gleaned from several different conflict resolution approaches and placed within a school/teacher/parent problem-solving context. These concepts were gleaned from these Web sites, which readers are encouraged to investigate: Integrated Curriculum for Achieving Necessary Skills (http://www.literacynet.org/icans/chapter03/steps.html); Learning Peace (http://www.learningpeace.com/pages/LP_04.htm); Mediation Works (http://www.mediation-works.org/pg4.cfm); and Office of Human Resource Development, University of Wisconsin–Madison (http://www.ohrd.wisc.edu/onlinetraining/resolution/index.asp).

ELEVEN GLOBAL APPROACHES TOWARD CONFLICT RESOLUTION

1. *Choose a "safe" place or as neutral a site as possible for the discussion and a time when both parties are more relaxed.*

It is customary to have parents come to the school for parent-teacher conferences. However, the school site, and most specifically the classroom, is not a neutral site to the parent because of who works there. Educators may want to consider an alternate site within the school building that the resistant parent may perceive as more "parent friendly" than the teacher's "home turf." Is there a conference room that is reserved specifically for such meetings and is not "owned" by the educator? Is there another office setting, such as the school counselor's office, in which the parent might feel more comfortable knowing that a third party was present to help negotiate what is about to occur? Such things are important to consider in helping create the optimum "safe" setting for the parent who is known to be uncooperative. Every opportunity that is provided to neutralize the resistant parent's concerns is one less stumbling block that will have to be dealt with as the problem-solving process moves forward.

2. *All parties need to be calm at the start of the discussion of sensitive issues.*

This atmosphere is best achieved by avoiding "drop-in" visits from parents or setting up conferences with parents on the day that some kind of unsettling incident has occurred. Educators who care about their students are just as prone to being upset with misbehaviors among his or her charges as the average person—perhaps even more so! No one in his or her right mind wants to see children mistreat each other. Time is a great modifier of emotions for everyone. Parents who show up unexpectedly in the heat of some kind of bullying situation may be operating from more of an emotional state than a rational one. Likewise, we may have our own issues to resolve regarding our feelings toward a child who is the constant purveyor of mayhem against peers.

It is often helpful for parents to know as much as possible in advance about what is on the agenda when the educator schedules the meeting. It is also often helpful to remember Point 1 above about the importance of neutral, nonthreatening sites for the parent. The more that can be done to defuse a tense situation, the less likely a meeting will be to spiral out of control when the tough issues begin to arise during discussions. The teacher must maintain a calm manner throughout the conference, even when parents begins to lose their decorum. If parents choose to "lose it" in a conference, that is *their* choice. We cannot fall for that distracting tactic, lest we be leveraged into *their* game. If a parent becomes unreasonable to the point of engaging in threatening behaviors, then the educator is best served to end the conference as soon as possible and seek whatever assistance may be needed.

3. *Identify the problem to be discussed and stay on task.*

How will we get where we are going if we don't have a road map? Identification of the issues to be discussed *is* the road map of problem solving in conflict resolution. It is helpful to the parent if these items can be identified before the conference is held. Such identification of issues may help lessen a parent's anxiety about what is going to occur during the conference. Parents will want to know what is so important that they have to be summoned to the Teacher's Court for judgment over their child, especially if they need to take time off from work for the meeting.

If there is not a *standard protocol* in a school for handling teacher-parent conferences, it will help increase a *sense of trust* if the ground rules for the conference can be developed between the parent and the teacher. It is much better to say, "While we're here to discuss some concerns about Katie's behaviors over the past few weeks, I would also like to know what *you* would like to get out of this conversation," rather than say to the parent (who already doesn't like us, remember?), "We're here to talk about Katie's behaviors over the past few weeks and what you're going to have to do at home to make her stop acting that way."

The most effective way to increase the chances of success for the conference is to follow the **basic respect ground rule**: "While we may disagree over what we are about to discuss, we want to make sure that we talk to each other respectfully and clearly so that we don't get sidetracked. I'm sure you are as upset in your own right about having to have this meeting as I am, but what we're both here to do is to help Julie become more successful at school." The basic respect ground rule will pay dividends when the going gets tough later on.

4. *Respect each other.*

To increase the chances of everyone being heard, respect must be at the heart of the conflict resolution process. The old adage that "we can agree to disagree" is predicated on a foundation of respect. An educator doesn't have to agree with the parent—and vice versa—but if some kind of solution is going to emerge from the problem-solving process, both parties must agree to at least *respect the process* of trying to come to a compromise, if not respecting each other. It helps if the parties come to like each other before having to work together to solve a complicated problem.

That respect can be stated at the outset, as was done in Point 3. The same ground rule of respect that is established at the outset can be the anchor to which we can return when a discussion gets stormy: "Let's remember our basic ground rule, Mr. Leny. We agreed that we would be less likely to be able to work together if we made nasty comments about each other. Thanks." A parent who is not used to having to act in a respectful manner toward others may need guidance to help bring those attributes into play. People are never too old to learn—both parents *and* educators. What we don't want to do is use our position of authority in a condescending manner toward a parent who is slipping out of control, since it will likely bring that parent straight back to behaviors that he or she knows best. If uncooperative and combative parents feel threatened, they are likely to return the favor, disengage from the conversation, or leave the conference.

And one last thing. *Respect has to be earned; it is not granted by virtue of position or authority.* Parents who are skeptical about educators may well have learned to be that way because of how they were treated in the past. What better way to gain more cooperative parents than to act counter to the way they thought we would: "Rather than being abrasive and condescending like all the others, this teacher seems to really care about my kid and what I think. Maybe I'll give her a better chance the next time we talk."

5. *Each side must listen.*

This is one of the most difficult parts of conflict resolution. Each side must be willing to *actually listen* to the other party. To do so means having to give up many of those cherished preconceived notions about who that other person sitting on the other side of the table is. The "mean father" may actually be disciplining his children the only way he knows how and may be telling us that he needs help with new ideas on how to handle his home situation. The "neglectful mother" may be telling us that she is so overwhelmed by conditions in her life that she has simply given up and now just lets her children do what they want because she doesn't have the energy to keep up with them anymore. What is this parent actually saying to me? What is it about this parent's story that will help make things better?

Listening, of course, must go beyond just the words used by the parent. Voice tone, assuredness of presentation, and body language all communicate too. But the main focus of communication may need to *stay on the content* of what is said since, in the end, it is that content that must be put into some kind of plan for everyone to follow. We don't have to like the way a parent voices what is said since we won't be translating that attitude into our behavior with the child. If the parent is willing to work within the framework of what everyone agreed to and toward a goal of making things better, I really don't care how crude and objectionable I may personally find the presentation—what I'm after is results!

6. *Speak professionally and use statements that are clear.*

If we listen well, it will help us formulate better plans. One way to do this with minimal confusion is to speak clearly and say exactly what is meant to be said. Although the various conflict resolution approaches have their own ways of accomplishing this goal, they virtually all seem to agree on the need to *speak from an "I" perspective.* "You" statements are usually taken as condemnations and tend to put people on the defensive: "You told me that you'd talk to Jenny about her behaviors. Can't you do anything that you said you would?" Ouch.

"I" statements may have to include some "yous" in them, but the "I" *demonstrates the partnership* of the collaborative effort and the "yous" are not used in a condemning fashion: "I was hoping that you would be able to talk to Jenny about her behaviors since that will increase my ability to be successful with her here at school. Is there something that I can do to help you accomplish what we agreed to last week?"

"I" statements are generally more honest too. We don't really know what that difficult parent is thinking; we just like to think we do: "You just did that to make sure that this plan wouldn't work." We can, however, talk about our own thoughts and feelings: "I have to share with you, Mrs. Pepper, that I am disappointed that the plan we drew up last week hasn't worked. It makes me feel as if I somehow missed something while we were designing it. Is there something I can do to increase the chances that it might work this week?" Using "I" statements with parents who are skeptical about school personnel shows a greater depth of commitment to problem solving than these parents are accustomed to.

We must also be willing to *use clear language* with parents so that there is no misinterpretation of something that we might say in "eduspeak." This statement is clear: "We cannot allow George to continue to keep hitting others on the playground. It isn't fair to other students. It violates school rules. We need your help if we are going to be able to avoid having to suspend him because of his behavior." Those words are *precise, accurate,* and *focused.* There is no uncertainty about what they mean to both parent and teacher.

7. *Identify points of agreement when possible to create a sense of cooperation and success.*

Nothing succeeds like success! So, let's try to make it happen as soon as possible in the problem-solving process before we get bogged down over the sticky issues that, undoubtedly, are going to come up. The likelihood of getting to that **win-win position** (Drew, 2002) that we want increases each time both parties feel as if they are successful in moving toward their goals. In most conflicts, there are certain items that are low-threat to both parties. They are likely to be small matters, but each successful small step will help both parties leverage toward the middle where the real work must be done.

So, what are some of those little agreements that might work toward calming down a skeptical parent? Both of you are working together to solve a problem with a child about whom you both care; are concerned about helping that child's overall school experience improve; are trying to avoid things getting worse; are trying to learn about each other; and are willing to listen to each other's points of view. What about some concrete, low-threat common denominators? Identify some traits of the child who is creating the problem that are positive, that provide alternative viewpoints to the problem behaviors, and that indicate that the child is capable of acting in ways that are not always viewed as negative. Heck, comment on the child's taste in clothes or music, if that's what it takes to make some kind of positive connection with the parent! Who cares, as long as we can find *something* positive to agree on with the parent as soon as possible to keep the parent interested in staying around for the "good stuff."

8. *Identify points of disagreement and work toward compromise.*

This is the aforementioned "good stuff." Point 8 is the most difficult part of the conflict resolution process, and it is where all the earlier elements come into play to increase the likelihood that the parent will hang around for the main event. This is where the uncooperative parent may come into full stride and the hurricane may want to wreak havoc across the marsh. However, if Points 1 through 7 have worked—both parties feel secure and safe, are calm, agree on the goals to be accomplished, have been listening to one another, are speaking honestly and clearly, and have identified several positive items of common ground early on—then working on the difficult issues may not turn out to be as difficult as both parties fear.

A key variable in working on the tough stuff is the ability of both parties to be *flexible* and *willing to compromise.* Win-win means no lose-lose or win-lose. Win-win is actually in the middle of either of those last two possibilities. Compromise demands the willingness of both sides to bend, to be willing to give up something of value for the greater good. Both sides will likely have to lose-lose and trade off win-loses to get to win-wins. If one party or the other is inflexible and refuses to "give in order to get," then true compromise cannot occur and both parties are likely to feel as if they got little, if anything, from their efforts.

One method of dealing with disagreements is to agree that the stumbling blocks may require more time to solve than the more readily achievable points of agreement noted in Point 7. Time is critical and can provide both parties with different insights if they have the luxury and willingness to meet over a period of time, rather than just for a single problem-solving session.

Write out the points of disagreement so that both parties can see if the words actually describe the situation. Sometimes we get hung up on particular verbiage to the exclusion of working on the real problem. Once the actual disagreements are described, it helps if both parties will identify what they would be willing to give up to move toward the middle ground. Again, a stubborn parent who chooses not to do this will likely sink the boat of bargaining. However, it is also important to recognize that all parties may not be willing to compromise on all items under discussion. If there are four disagreements on the table and the parent-teacher conference yields compromise on three of them, I'd call that a fairly successful mediation of differences. Let's just hope that the first disagreement discussed doesn't turn out to be the one that the parent refuses to bend on, for that will set the stage for all of the other items on the table to follow.

9. *Commit to the plan.*

Once a compromise plan has been developed, it is important for both parties to be able to review it in some written form, even if that format in the short run is the roughest of drafts. "Seeing" a written plan allows both parties to do last-minute troubleshooting and tweaking. Also, it prevents one side or the other from leaving the room with false impressions about exactly what was agreed to since the final agreement is there for all to see.

Commitment to the plan requires two things. First, there must be the aforementioned *agreement between parent and educator on the main points* of what is supposed to occur. Second, both sides must indicate verbally, if not in writing by initialing the draft, their *willingness to try* to make the plan work. By indicating that willingness to try, both parties have committed themselves to move forward and must know exactly what their individual roles will be, which leads us to the next point.

10. *Identify responsibilities.*

Parents and educators need to be clear on exactly what it is that they are to do once the conference is over and the plan begins. This can be done in the planning stage by actually identifying the party who has the specific responsibility to do each item designated in the written plan and entering that person's initials beside the task. It is important to ensure that both educator and parent have approximately the same number of items identified so that one party does not feel overburdened with more responsibilities than the other as the actual work begins. If a parent ends up with more responsibilities than the teacher, the parent must understand why the plan is designed that way and how it will work to the child's advantage. At all costs, we must avoid "dumping" a ton of responsibilities on parents without them understanding the reason and, more important, being willing to accept the challenges. If anything, the educator should try to *show good faith* in the plan by being willing to accept "just one more" task assignment than the parent.

Points 9 and 10 work best when they are employed simultaneously. A party actually should not commit to a task if it is one that seems "untryable" to that individual. Educators may have to encourage parents to "give it a couple of tries" in order to see that the task *is* actually achievable, since they may well be exhausted from trying other approaches and not have the stomach to attempt something else that they think will fail too.

It is best to *use exact language* in identifying who is responsible for which tasks. *Too many plans fail because of nonspecific assignments*: "Okay, I feel really good that we were able to meet today to discuss this and draw up a plan. Let me know how your part goes." As with the guidelines given in Chapter 5, specificity increases the likelihood of a plan's success: "I feel so much better after our discussion and planning today. Now, let me make certain that I know which parts of this plan I'm supposed to do, and which ones you'll be working on. Okay, I'm doing items 3, 4, and 5. You'll be working on 1, 2, 6, and 7, and we'll both be working on 4 and 5. Does that sound right to you?" Each review of the plan increases the likelihood of success as it decreases the chances of misunderstanding the roles each party is to play in the implementation process.

11. *Follow through.*

As with garbled communication, another failure of efforts to make plans work is the lack of follow-through by one or both parties. Follow-through does four things. It reminds the agents of change that the plan is still in operation: "We seem to have been successful with our first three steps. What's next on our list?" It allows one side to ask the other for advice or assistance if it is experiencing difficulty implementing the plan: "In all honesty, I've had trouble with what we agreed to do for step two. I wonder if you have any advice on how I might approach that item from a different angle." Furthermore, it continues to refresh the parties' minds as to what their responsibilities are: "Now let's see. I've managed to work through the first three steps. How are you coming along with your first three?" Perhaps most important, it identifies areas that might need modification as the plan moves along: "It seems as if we have been successful up to item 5 on our list, but after that things don't seem to be working as well as they did. Do you think we need to meet again to revamp our plan?"

Follow-through is essential on both the parent's and the educator's part. It increases the level of communication between the home and school environment. Both sides know that, no matter how they may be uncertain each about other, they *will* be talking together again in the future, so it just might be nice if they had some successes to talk about in light of whatever else they may think of one another. Follow-through with the parent who is struggling sends a compassionate message of hope that there really *is* someone else out there who cares about improving the situation with the child who is difficult. Follow-through also makes it clear to parents that they have certain responsibilities to keep the plan moving ahead. A parent's agreement to a plan is not the end of the parent's responsibility. A successful plan requires that *both* the parent and the teacher work hard to make it a reality.

It is often easy, however, for educators to forget to follow through with interventions because of the massive amount of work that we have to do. We often arrange our lives around checking off the list of a thousand things that must be done in order to plow ahead with the next one, never pausing to go back and see how many of those things need additional attention or modification. We keep plunging ahead toward that next set of tasks to be accomplished because, if we dare come up for air, we'll be inundated with still more work, which will just make us run faster in our little hamster cages.

Although that may be the nature of the educational system, and there may truly be some things that we can do that require little follow-through, we have to prioritize those situations that require additional time and fight to ensure that we get the resources we need to fulfill them. Time is that most precious commodity of which we usually have so little, and it is that very thing that we need to request more of so that we can do more prevention work. Such is the very nature of what we do when we provide follow-through on intervention plans.

Chapter Seven

Types of Difficult Parents

There are many different categories of personalities that parents bring with them into our conferences. Isn't *that* a nice way to say it! We often learn very quickly where the child has learned the behavior under discussion.

Although there are various descriptions of difficult people that we can find from different sources, one of the most appropriate and useful sets of categories that I have found comes from the Ohio Literacy Resource Center (see http://literacy .kent.edu). The focus of the project Web page, entitled "Working With Difficult People," is on difficult workplace personalities; however, the basic styles of inter-action it describes are useful in helping us design responses to parents who seem to sabotage parent-teacher conferences. So, with all appropriate credit due the source for its inspiration, let's take some basic templates and see how those per-sonality types apply to working with difficult parents.

THE PARENT BULLY

The most obvious type of parent we might expect to encounter in working with children who bully others are those who have taught them everything they know. These are the parents who are used to getting what they want in public by raising their voices and using physical posturing in ways to intimidate others. They are careful not to cross the lines into violating the law—after all, they aren't likely to physically assault a teacher—but they are also not adverse to operating right beneath the lines of behavior that might get them into trouble with authority.

The Parent Bully will likely be the most objectionable type of parent we encounter. Parent Bullies probably do not have any great love for school per-sonnel. They may tolerate us just until they can determine a way to leverage the discussion their way. They expect to be in charge, so taking power away from them is a frightening prospect. As a result, they are likely to fight hard to maintain con-trol of the conference in whatever way they deem necessary so as not to feel intim-idated themselves.

A wise approach with Parent Bullies is to recognize their need for power and avoid outright confrontations with them that would give the impression that the goal of the conference is to take their power away. *Steering the conference early toward neutral conversational territory* is important. Is there something that the educator has in common with this parent? *Finding commonalities* is essential in working with difficult people as it increases the opportunities to lower their defenses. When common ground is established, the Parent Bully may feel less compelled to use domination as the central tool for discussion. It is more difficult for them to intimidate someone they like.

Do not be afraid of Parent Bullies. Fear is exactly the tool they are accustomed to using. Expect to feel some uneasiness when dealing with them, however. There will likely be some evolutionary hardwiring that we cannot avoid. Our bodies will probably be more alert than if we were teaching first-grade reading. We may realize that our hearts are beating a little faster than normal along with suddenly noticing in the middle of everything that our necks are stiff. Our bodies are getting ready to fight, flee, or freeze. A helpful trick when discovering that relaxation is in order is to monitor our breathing. When we are tense, we breathe shallowly from the upper chest. When we breathe more deeply, it sends more oxygen throughout the body and helps us calm down. Let's let the Parent Bully be the one who grows befuddled, if anyone has to be that way. We'll stay in the driver's seat by keeping the cooler head.

Sometimes we find that Parent Bullies are not actually as ferocious as the reputation that precedes them. The rumor mill and the child's stories may paint a picture of a person far worse than the ogre we end up encountering. Take the parent at face value from what you observe during the interaction. Parent Bullies may not live up to their reputation in your presence. *You* may have the magic touch. Also, keep in mind that sometimes Parent Bullies are really those exhausted parents I mentioned earlier who are eager for assistance in helping them deal with *l'enfant terrible*. Like Aesop's fable of the Lion and the Shepherd, Parent Bullies may be more than willing to repay kindness when it is given to them instead of the stereotypical "bad parent" response they expect to receive from school personnel.

THE SILENT TREATMENT

The Silent Treatment is the parent who either has little to say or chooses to say little as a method to make the educator do all the work. The parent who doesn't respond from a position of not knowing what to say or from deference to the teacher (as was the case with Mr. Rojas) is one who can often be nurtured by our compassion and kindness into becoming a more-than-willing partner in the mutual problem-solving process. It's the Silent Treatment that emerges from a basis of obstinacy or hostility that poses the greater challenge for educators. That's the kind of parent we focus on here.

When faced with the Silent Treatment, educators have a tendency to do what they do best—keep talking! That is exactly what Silent Treatment wants. As long as *we* do the talking, *they* have no investment in the topic or plan. "Well, it was *your* idea," is the basic response from Silent Treatment to a plan that is in trouble or fails. If we fall for that setup, then we deserve the "credit." Never make a plan for two people that is one-sided.

Silent Treatments will respond only when they have to, so let's give them a reason to respond! If it becomes apparent early on that we are facing the Silent Treatment Challenge, then call them on it:

> *Mr. Gno, what we are trying to do here today is work on a plan that both of us will end up following. I cannot do that without your input or opinion. Actually, I won't do that without your input because I consider you to be a teammate in helping to solve the problems that have brought us here in the first place. If I could solve the problem myself, it would have been done long ago—that's why I'm turning to you now. I need your insight.*

Silent Treatments are used to controlling the situation by their lack of responses. When they do nothing, others have to do all the work. The power of the Silent Treatments rests in their abilities to always be right. *They* never suggest anything, but they can certainly criticize *others* for what they don't like about a plan, an activity, or some other venture. From the Silent Treatments' perspective, nothing ventured *is* something gained! They maintain a position of superiority by not owning a part of a plan—if we let them get away with it:

> *Mr. Gno, one of the things we know about successful planning is that both parties have to be willing to contribute something to the final plan. Quite frankly, to this point, I feel as if I've been making all the suggestions about possible alternatives to Helen's behaviors. That doesn't make me feel like we're working together and I just simply have to have your input before I will move on. What is it that you would like to contribute or have thought about this process since you've been here today?*

A crafty approach with the Silent Treatments is something (anything!) to jump-start them toward joining in the conversation, even if what they say is a criticism of what is transpiring. If the Silent Treatments complain, at least we've got *something* to negotiate:

> *Okay, you've indicated that you don't like what we're doing. I'm open to any ideas you have. What directions do you think we should take? I'm eager to work with you in any way possible.*

The trick is always to keep the Silent Treatments engaged and maybe even provide a little positive provocation to get them to respond, as a method of increasing their participation.

THE STALLER

Stallers are one step ahead of Silent Treatments in that at least they have to communicate to be able to accomplish their mission. Stallers may balk at coming into school for the initial or follow-up conferences or may drag their feet about implementing the agreed-on plan, but at least they are telling us the "reasons" why they are stalling—maybe not the real reasons, but something that provides additional fodder for us to use to subvert their devious plans!

Stallers may do what their name implies because they are uncertain about exactly *what* or *how* they should carry out their part of the plan. Did we go over their parts of it in enough detail so that it was clear as to exactly what they need to do? Do they need additional assistance in understanding their role? Sometimes parents are hesitant because they are afraid of not being able to do their part successfully and don't want to disappoint school personnel. They are afraid that we will view them as even bigger "failures" than they feel they are now. These Stallers are far easier to work with since their hesitancy comes from a core of wanting to do good; they just need additional encouragement or assistance to move forward.

Other Stallers act as they do as a power-and-control mechanism—do you see a pattern emerging here among these difficult parents? By not moving forward into their parts of a plan or by moving more slowly than specified by the agreed-on timetable, they keep the leverage in their court since *our* ability to move is linked to *their* actually doing it! These Stallers require gentle persuasion in order to call them on their own game:

> *Mr. Gno, I just wanted to check with you again this week and see how things have been going at home. I really prefer not to keep checking in so much, but I wanted to remind you that we can't keep moving forward on our agreed-on plan until you let me know how your conversations with your daughter went. Is there something that I can do to help?*

The Staller responds with a list of "reasons" why he has not done his part of the plan.

> *Mr. Gno, I can understand how life often gets in the way of our plans, but in all honesty I have to share with you that I cannot improve the situation here at school until you take that first step on the plan we agreed to last week. If you would like to meet with me again to renegotiate something that will make it easier for you to get started, I will be more than happy to do that, but you have to understand that right now we're stuck with the same problems we had last week when you left and I can't guarantee that things will improve until you take that first step from home. I am willing to schedule a meeting with you after school any day this week. What do we need to do to help you take that first step?*

Shining the spotlight of accountability onto Stallers sends them a message that they are being "watched," something to which they are probably not used to having to respond. Knowing that their agreement to a plan is not enough—knowing that they are actually going to have to *do* it—changes the rules by which they are used to playing. Stallers stall because they get away with it. People get used to the idea that they cannot count on Stallers to do their parts of the bargain, so they end up expecting them to do just that—nothing. Keeping a constant, gentle pressure on Stallers can be one way to move them toward action since the thing that they want the most is for us to go away! When we don't go away, the Stallers must make a choice—either do *something* to make us go away or try on another personality mask to see if that will diminish our presence. We have to be persistent and patient with Stallers. We must be willing to outwait them with our diligence and commitment to the plan.

THE NEGATIVE

Negatives use their constant belief in the "no" to bog everything down. "It won't work" is their mantra. Nothing is ever good enough to solve the problem—the school is bad, the teachers are bad, life is unfair, their children never get a fair shake. Negatives are particularly tricky when it comes to getting them to participate in any planning since, as they know (and have probably already told you), no matter what comes out of the conference, it isn't going to work.

Like Stallers, Negatives require persistence and patience to wait out their usual negative plan of attack. It is sometimes helpful when we "acknowledge" the Negative's beliefs in the difficulty of life:

> *Mr. Gno, I agree totally with you. It is very difficult to raise kids today. It's also really tough to work with them in the classroom. That's why we believe in teaming up with parents to work together to solve the problems like we've had the last few weeks with Helen. Because of many of the same reasons you've pointed out about the difficulties in raising and teaching children today, we know that it takes a team of parents and teachers working with children both at home and at school to untangle some of the messes that they get themselves into.*

Negatives are used to using their toxicity to poison the atmosphere of planning. Remember, to Negatives, *nothing* will work. *Nothing.* That also includes them—if we let them get away with it. By initially buying into the Negatives' views about the difficulties of life, we are temporarily aligning ourselves with their world of woe and misery, but just to pique their curiosity enough that they won't exclude us from further interaction. Curiosity kills the cat, right? We are trying to get them to keep their doors open long enough so that we can convince them to give us another shot—if for nothing else so that, from their point of view, they can keep their doors open long enough to bend our ears some more about how nothing ever works. Hey, I'll continue to be the audience for that if I think that, in the long run, I'll eventually wear them down and they will commit to a plan that is going to improve the situation.

> *Mr. Gno, I've listed all the reasons you've given me today as to why you believe that a plan to improve your daughter's behaviors here at school won't work. I think that we can address many of your concerns, and I'd like to respond right now to each one of them before we move forward to making that plan.*

Negative Parents win because they are used to educators giving up under their tidal waves of negativism. If they can convince us how useless it is to even start, then their worldview remains intact. See, they were right. Not only is everything bad, it's so bad that even *we* won't try to solve the problem after they have informed us of how bad things really are. Oh, woe. Oh, misery. Oh—what garbage!

We deal with Negatives by allowing them to vent their frustrations, addressing those concerns as best we can and then coaxing them into moving forward on a plan:

Mr. Gno, in spite of everything that you believe about why planning won't work, would you be willing to commit to just one mutually agreed on thing to try at home to see if it works? Just one. I think I know something that Helen will like and that you'll be pleasantly surprised at how well she responds to it. Give me a shot with this one task for you to do at home and then we'll meet again next week to review how things are going. If that one works, then we can discuss several other things that might work too. If it doesn't, then you can come back and tell me how wrong I was and we'll discuss what went wrong and still try to pick out several other things that might work in the future. Are you willing to at least work with me on that?

With this gambit, the educator had better *know* up front something that is a virtual 100% guaranteed success with the child since the Negative Parent has a vested interest in even the smallest of plans not working. The fail-proof idea should be fun for the child, low-threat for the parent, and something that both of them will likely want to do.

THE COMPLAINER

Like several other difficult parent types, Complainers find fault with everything. They often come wrapped with a Negative Parent hidden inside just to make things more interesting. And just wait until Mr. Negative and Mrs. Complainer *both* show up as the parents of Attila the Child.

Complainers are critical. Whereas Negatives talk about how nothing works, Complainers whine. Things *may* work, but they don't work well enough. There is always something better out there than the current reality for Complainers. They can be loud, but not necessarily so. For the Complainer, the fun is in reminding us how nothing is ever perfect or in making us feel as if we are the failures by not being able to solve the problem in advance of the conference. Complainers often heap additional torment on educators by their insistence on providing criticism about the least little something that goes astray. They hide behind a cloak of perfectionism, but perfection is not what they really want. They use that perfectionism as a weapon to club any plan to death, and they will jump side to side, forward, backward, and even up in the air to avoid agreeing that something actually does work. It's quite a sight to behold.

We outsmart Complainers with many of the same approaches that we use with Negatives. Agreeing with Complainers from the outset about the imperfections of the world is always a good start. It helps take the wind out of their sails. Of course, with their endless supply of air, they continue to blow the ship of success onto the rocks even after we give them a little satisfaction just to humor them as we try to keep the doors of communication open:

Mr. Gno, it's clear to me that you have a high degree of expectations for our school. We agree on that, although we may disagree about exactly which things we might need to emphasize all the time. It's clear to me that we both agree that we want the best for your daughter. That's why we're here today. Everything we plan might not work the way we both think it should, but I believe that our mutual commitment to excellence will at least make a big dent in solving the problems that we're here to discuss.

Complainers can often be outwitted by allowing them to incorporate their complaints into the plan. We can turn the tables (subvert their dominant paradigm) on Complainers by allowing *them* to work on those items about which they seem to be most upset:

It's very clear to me that you are concerned about several types of behaviors that we've talked about today. I wonder if you would be willing to work on three specific kinds of behaviors at home with Helen? It seems as if the loud voice, the disrespectful behavior toward her friends, and the pushing and shoving are three things that you can talk to her about from home. Tell her your concerns about how these behaviors make you feel as a parent. You mentioned to me that you feel as if her behavior is a reflection on you. I think now's a good time to discuss this with her and reinforce those values you've shared with me that you and your wife have instilled in her. If you can talk to her about just those three things—three things that we both agree are important and that we want to try and stop—that will help us work together as we try and solve this issue.

Notice that in the dialogue above, the parent had expressed a criticism of his own child. Complainers are equal opportunity whiners. Even their own children may receive the wrath of the whining parent. Never be surprised by what you hear coming from the mouths of Complainers. Of course, they likely will start eating their own children only *after* they've exhausted all other food supplies in the room (specifically *you*), all the other teachers, the school district, and the greater society. A part of the strategy in dealing with Complainers is to take away their "food supply" until the only things left to focus on in a discussion begin to "go home." Once we begin to spin the discussion so that the Complainer has no other place or person to criticize except those closer to home, we are likely to be on the road to "wearing them down" toward making a plan. In the end, we can work with only those people over whom we have direct control:

I hear your frustration over all the confusion in the world which helps to influence poor behavioral choices with our kids. I don't disagree with you on many of your points. In fact, I could probably add a few to the list! But I know that, in the long run, the only people that can truly make the changes we need to make sometimes are the individuals themselves. Parents and teachers play a huge role in influencing our kids to make better decisions and that's what we're trying to do by this plan—convince your daughter of the wisdom of making those changes. We can critique and criticize the world for all its ills all we want to, but in the end, we still have got to work together to solve these problems or things most likely won't improve.

Countering their moves and co-opting them into turning their complaints into solutions are the keys to working with Complainers.

KNOW-IT-ALLS

Know-It-Alls can do our jobs. Just ask them. Well, you really won't have to ask them because they will make it abundantly clear from the beginning of a conference, if they haven't already done so before their arrival.

Know-It-Alls may actually know a lot. Approach them from that angle. Know-It-Alls become problems when they think that their knowledge and solutions are superior to anything that anyone else has to offer. This is particularly vexing when the attitude is demeaning toward the educator. It is tough enough having to work with a gobzillion kids all day long without having Know-It-Alls come in and tell us how dumb we really are!

Like Complainers, Know-It-Alls need to be co-opted into any plan that is developed since they are likely to have a high degree of ownership if the plan reflects their wisdom as opposed to ours:

> *Mr. Gno, I have to tell you, you really have a lot of ideas that you've brought to the table today. It's clear to me that you've thought a great deal about all of this. I wish every parent that I meet with put in as much thought as you have on solving problems. This looks like we'll be able to develop a plan in no time!*

Know-It-Alls need to have their egos massaged. A great way to do that is to give them credit for their ideas, even if those ideas are unworkable. As with brainstorming, the more ideas on the table, the greater the likelihood of *something* working. Hey, remember, it could be worse—you could be "talking" with a Silent Treatment! Know-It-Alls may actually have some workable ideas, and if they do, don't fail to include them in the plan. The trick is to convince Know-It-Alls that any plan that is developed is a collaborative effort, and that means that both the teacher and the parent will have input into the final plan. Appeal to their superior wisdom:

> *I know that you are aware that the most effective plans are those that include the best ideas from different points of view.*

> or

> *Your ideas are really helpful. It will make it easier to include some of them into our final plan.*

> or

> *This is really great that you have brought with you all of these possibilities on how to help solve this problem. You've been doing some homework on this, I can tell. You'll find it a breeze to work on the plan that we end up developing together.*

Unlike Complainers, who just like to carp about how bad things are, Know-It-Alls most often have ideas about how to "fix" things. They may be wrong, but they've got plenty to offer, nonetheless. It is important to make certain that Know-It-Alls "know" that you are listening to them. Whether you agree or disagree is not the point. The point is that they expect that their opinions will be heard because they are "smart."

Avoid assuming that Know-It-Alls have little useful to add to the planning process just because they have a grating personality. We have to make certain that we don't automatically turn off *our* ears just because we have a parent in the room who punches our buttons. Unless there is some other solution out there (translated: someone else solves the problem for us!), we're going to have to work with Know-It-All Parents, so we might as well figure out a way to help them learn to work with us sooner rather than later.

ANGELS

There are Angels among us! And they are quite interesting to work with too.

Angel Parents may, indeed, be sweet, kind-hearted, and well meaning. They can also be two-faced. It's important to know which ones show up for the conference before we can develop a plan that is likely to be most effective.

True Angels want good things to happen for all involved. The problem is that they may not have the resources or intestinal fortitude to do their part to make them happen. They don't have a disciplining bone in their bodies when it comes to managing their children, or they may actually have lost control of them through no fault of their own. They may be compliant and agreeable during the conference from a position of respect to the educator. They may not be accustomed to speaking up when they need to in order to be heard. The goodwill is there, but the ability to carry through may not be.

True Angels need to be encouraged. They need to know that it is okay to offer ideas (definitely *not* the problem for the Know-It-Alls!) and ask questions. If they are timid about their parenting role, let them know that their help is a good thing:

Your being here today is a really positive sign. It's important that we have your input into this plan even if you believe that what you might offer won't help. I believe it will. Never underestimate your ability to be a strong parent. Your willingness to speak up at home with your daughter is very important and will go a long way toward helping solve this problem.

Then there are the other Angels—the two-faced ones. Two-Faced Angels hide behind a mask of cooperation when their real goal is to sabotage any plan that is placed before them. They live behind the façade of being willing to do whatever it takes to help make the solution work without having any intention of doing so. They may engage in some of the tactics of the Staller in failing to do their parts. Similar to the Negatives, they typically will have lots of excuses about why they cannot complete their responsibilities—and they're *nice,* too, as they explain their reasoning.

Seeing through the veil of a Two-Faced Angel and calling him or her on it are keys to success:

Mr. Gno, I have to share with you some frustration I have about what you've shared with me as reasons for your not talking with Helen about the things we agreed on in the plan. I'm really getting a mixed message. You assure me when we meet that you will do your part, but then when we meet the next week nothing seems to have been accomplished. Last week we reviewed the plan and ironed out those things which you indicated were problematic and I looked forward to hearing all the good things that were going to occur after you did your part. I'm beginning to wonder how much success we're going to have if either one of us doesn't do what we agreed we would. What is it that needs to happen to make our plan work?

Confrontation with a recalcitrant parent doesn't have to be threatening, although usually the individual who is being asked to explain a behavior might feel uncomfortable. In this instance, the confrontation merely (and nicely) points out what the teacher's frustration is and what the prognosis seems to be if one party or the other fails to do his or her part. Notice that the teacher keeps the focus on the positive by telling the parent that it was going to be a highlight to hear about the good things that occurred when the parent implemented his part of the plan. It was not condemning or accusatory. The teacher reminds the Two-Faced Angel that if either of them doesn't do their jobs, the plan most likely will not work, and concludes by asking for additional help from the parent to understand exactly what needs to be done to make "our plan" work. Avoid giving the parent a reason to abandon ship because you pushed them overboard, no matter how badly you really might want to do so!

WHAT ABOUT MEDIATION AND NEGOTIATION?

These typologies are a simplification of many different parent personalities that we are likely to meet in our daily work. Although these scenarios offer wonderful solutions to the perfect world created here, we all know that real life is much more unpredictable.

In the end, nothing might work with any of these parents. Then what? Sometimes we just have to admit that, in spite of all our grand skills as educators, some parents just will not follow the rule book. We must always ensure, however, that *we* are not the ones who give them the reason to throw in the towel. Difficult parents often look for reasons to bail when the tough work with their children lands back on their doorsteps. We must always be one step ahead of difficult parents and assume—sometimes in spite of evidence to the contrary—that they really *do* want to make things better. They just haven't learned yet how much better their lives will be when they listen more to *us* than to their own excuses that they have been making for all these years.

In the last chapter, we spoke of efforts to get to that win-win position with difficult people. There are many excellent resources to help educators adapt mediation and negotiation techniques to their repertoire of skills.

When two or more parties enter into some type of problem-solving situation in which both want the outcome to favor their position, a **negotiation** ensues. Negotiation, by nature, implies that some kind of conflict exists (Gerzon, 2006). Dana (2001) notes that there are two types of negotiations. In *power-based negotiations,* two or more parties are in adversarial positions from the outset. Neither side is fond of the other because of a dispute, disagreement, or shortage of resources. Needless to say, a power-based negotiation starts out with a higher tension level between the parties. It is almost inherently a win-lose situation. *Interest-based negotiations*, on the other hand, recognize that there is some kind of common good emerging from the process of resolving the issue at hand. Interest-based negotiations result in those precious win-win outcomes that we discussed in the previous chapter. They are not adversarial by nature since all parties involved are seeking a positive outcome. The negotiation may be over the degree or amount of the positive outcome. It is important to remember, particularly in the case of interest-based negotiations, that adversity or acrimony do not have to be in play for a negotiation to be successful. Unfortunately, as Dana notes, too often individuals involved in the discussion of difficult issues think that "being non-adversarial is being weak" (p. 41). It is important to remember that, even in the midst of difficult bargaining, "negotiators are people first" (Fisher, Ury, & Patton, 1991, p. 18).

As might be expected, power-based negotiations often end up being unpleasant experiences for all involved. Quite often, they bog down in an intractable, World War I-type trench warfare mentality in which each party would rather fight to the death than surrender position. When this situation occurs, outside help is usually needed. **Mediation** is a negotiation strategy that involves the intervention of a *third party* into the discussion between two parties who seem to be "stuck" (Moore, 2003). The third party who enters into the discussion is someone who is considered neutral to both of the competing sides—say a teacher and a parent—and someone without a vested interest in either side "winning." In most school settings, an effective mediator is the school counselor who has the skills by virtue of education to enter the realm of a conflict and seek solutions without bias toward either side. The mediator has no vested interest in a "win-lose" outcome for the parties; subsequently, the role of the mediator is to craft meetings between the conflicting sides in ways that allow the principals involved to avoid the pitfalls that have prevented them from reaching a solution up to that point.

Mediation, with the right person, has a high probability of some type of resolution—not that either party will be completely satisfied, but then that is not the purpose of mediation. Kressel (2006) notes that the median success rate for some type of mediated resolution to a conflict is approximately 60% (p. 728). This rate is quite phenomenal when one considers that prior to the intervention by a mediator, the success rate of the parties at loggerheads is zero! The effective mediator is one who "stays out of the minefield"—the mediator structures the meetings so that the parties in conflict do most of the work, hence increasing ownership of the ultimate agreements.

The bottom line to working with difficult parents is to know when to negotiate and when to consider mediation. Don't let the power struggle and ownership of an idea get in the way of a child's education, which, unfortunately, is too often what happens when adults (who should know better) find themselves on opposite sides of a problem.

CHAPTER EIGHT

Helping Parents Talk at Home With Their Children About Misbehaviors

How can parents and educational personnel work together to improve the learning environment for every child, victim and bully alike? What can educators say to parents to increase the likelihood that they will talk to their children when they are involved in bullying others at school?

This section of the book is designed to be used by educators to help parents create better avenues for talking with their children about bullying. It is written *for* educators to be used *by* educators. It is *not* written for parents since it looks at the problem through the eyes of those in the classroom who are faced with coming up with ideas to offer parents during parent-educator discussions on the sensitive issue of school intimidation. It provides suggestions on approaches that educators can offer to parents to try with their children. Educators may find it useful, however, to create a handout of their own list of some of the main points and ideas discussed here to give to parents during such discussions.

First, let us review several barriers that often get in the way of our children telling us when they need assistance from their parents or teachers. One of the biggest stumbling blocks is the fear of what will happen to them if they do ask for assistance, especially if what they need help with is to discuss something that they have done that they know was wrong.

HELPING PARENTS UNDERSTAND PUNISHMENT, ACCOUNTABILITY, AND RESTITUTION

As we have noted, the bully has historically been portrayed as a victim of the home environment, although in today's world, **imitative aggression** from sources in the media is fast overtaking that traditional breeding ground of bullies. This is not to be misinterpreted in any way as implying that bullies should not be held accountable for their actions because of the absorption from that aforementioned osmosis of violence. Let us be very clear on this fact with parents: *bullies are to be held accountable for their actions.* Failure to do so is an abdication of adult responsibility. But receiving punishment of some sort for misbehavior (which may be in order as a part of an intervention) is not the same as being held accountable, nor does punishment in and of itself provide avenues for efforts to make up for the harm done, a process called **restitution**. Holding the child accountable may be perceived by the individual being corrected as equivalent to a punishment, but that may be only a matter of interpretation on the part of the wrongdoer and more related to having been caught in the transgression.

Victims elicit a nurturing response within us, but it is harder for us to be empathetic with bullies. Indeed, the history of this country, as is legendary in film and literature on the settling of the "Wild West" with its concept of frontier justice, has taught us that the "bad guys always get what's coming to 'em," whether "what's coming to 'em" is at the end of a rope or a shootout with a stubby-cigar-smoking Clint Eastwood. The need for revenge, to even the score, and for the guilty party to be punished, people think, is an almost reflexive and biological demand. Such is the motive behind the **revenge fantasies** that victims often harbor and act on against their aggressors (perpetrators of high-profile incidents of school violence often justify their actions through a mind-set of "I had no other choice"). Contrary to popular opinion, the desire to settle wrongs with wrongs of an equivalent punitive power and nature is a learned response and one that is as wrongheaded and often as cruel as the desire that motivates those who use naked aggression and power to get what they want in the first place.

What is needed in the face of the chaos created by bullies for their victims and the families of those victims is a rational, mature, adult response. There is no need to escalate an already unhealthy and unsatisfactory situation with additional tension and further unbridled emotional responses. If, as Schwartz et al. (1997) noted, one of the traits of aggressive children is their "frequent exposure to violence in the home and their experience as an object of physical abuse" (p. 672), then we do not want to contribute additional "reasons" for parents to continue to behave in this fashion toward their children.

So what is the answer to holding the agents of intimidation accountable for their actions?

Perhaps we must provide another perspective on what is best for all involved when it comes to righting wrongs. **Punishment** is designed to inflict a price or pain of such magnitude in response to an improper behavior that the misguided individual will associate the price or pain with the infraction and not do the misdeed again. It is assumed that the individual will understand the larger context and meaning of why the punishment was administered (generalization). For those who are slower to pick up on the idea, additional punishments at increasing levels of intensity or frequency are supposed to do the trick. Above all, keep the punishments coming and increase the level of penalty with each subsequent transgression—or so the thinking goes.

We all know it does not quite work that way. Nor does the opposite approach, trying to love the perpetrators into compliance. What works best is something in the middle, a "tough love" approach that ensures fair and comprehensible accountability for the agents of mayhem, an approach that helps bullies learn new patterns of behavior to respond to the frustration, anger, and desire for immediate gratification that drive them.

RESTORATIVE JUSTICE

Restorative justice strives to achieve what its name implies: to restore to all parties a sense of justice and wholeness. It desires to return the victim, and all other affected parties, to the state they were in before the wrong was committed.

One of the best descriptions of the basic principles of restorative justice comes via the work of a collaborative of educators at the Minnesota Department of Education (Anderson et al., 1998). These educators noted the benefits of applying a restorative approach to infractions occurring in the school setting, and their work has since been adopted by other organizations throughout the country. The Mennonite Conciliation Service (Amstutz, 2000) summarized that work, as shown in Figure 8.1.

Each time I read these principles, I get dizzy—in a good sort of way. Look at what is included in the concept! First, there is the recognition that a wrong to an individual has an impact on the greater community. Second, there is the effort to bring all affected and concerned parties—both individually and collectively— together to help in a solution. Third, there is the acknowledgment that both the individual and the community have a vested interest in solving the problem. Fourth, there is the admission that others outside the realm of traditional or invested authority may have ideas that can lead to positive outcomes. Fifth, not only the victim but also the individual who committed the infraction and the greater community are given a voice about the wrong. Last, there is the admission that traditional methods of solving problems may not always work and that perhaps something different might be more successful. And look at the positivity expressed in the principles. They talk of "opportunity," of ways to "regain control" of one's life, to be "responsible for . . . actions," and to be "part of the solution."

These principles are very exciting from a parent-teacher alliance standpoint, largely because they reflect what so often is *not* done in addressing peer abuse in schools. The principles of restorative justice are not just the stuff of lily-livered, bleeding hearts. Quite the opposite. These principles demand a much *higher* degree of commitment and involvement on the part of school personnel, the aggrieved, the aggressor, parents, and concerned parties within the greater school community than simply administering a punishment that, in all likelihood, only admonishes the guilty party for getting caught. The application of restorative justice is hard, deliberative work. It takes *time*. It takes *planning*. It requires *risk* on the part of all participants to publicly express concern for what has happened and accept responsibility for being a part of the solution.

Figure 8.1   How Restorative Justice Helps Everyone Right a Wrong

For the person or persons harmed:
- a choice in how they want to proceed
- an opportunity to speak out about what happened to them
- an opportunity to speak directly to the person who committed the harm
- an opportunity to have a voice in how to make things as right as possible
- a way to regain control

For the person or persons who have committed the harm:
- a chance to be held accountable to the person harmed
- a chance to be responsible for their actions
- a chance to be part of the solution
- an opportunity to be reintegrated into the community they have harmed

For the school community:
- a way to handle problems that otherwise are not dealt with because there is no clear understanding about what to do
- an acknowledgment of the harm done to the community
- an opportunity to hold person(s) responsible for the harm accountable in a personal way
- an opportunity to have a voice in the solution

For school administrators:
- a method to have several people involved in problem solving and solutions instead of just choosing prescribed consequences that are often judged as too harsh or too lenient
- an agreement by all parties to information disclosed as a result of a conference
- a voluntary agreement to participate in a restorative discipline process ensuring greater levels of participation
- another approach for situations where traditional methods of punishment have not proven appropriate or effective

See Amstutz, L. (2000, Spring). Where to From Here? *Conciliation Quarterly*, v. 19, p. 11, and Anderson, C., et al. (1998). *Restorative Measures: Respecting Everyone's Ability to Resolve Problems*, p. 2.

There is little education in punishment beyond the message, "If you are caught doing that again, you will get more of the same until you are sneaky enough to avoid being observed doing it." In punishment, there is no effort made to compel the instigators of harm to *think* about what they did or about how they would feel if someone had done the same to them. Certainly, there is no thought given to a method of righting the wrong. *Punishment is always the easiest route to addressing the guilty party.* Accountability, on the other hand, as exemplified via restorative justice, requires considerable time and effort when it is done effectively. Again, keep in mind that holding one accountable may well be *perceived* as a punishment. More likely, however, what perpetrators of harm often find so distasteful is actually having to come face-to-face with the true implications of their actions. Nothing can be more unsettling than a big dose of reality through the mirror, reflecting truth about who we truly are and what we actually do.

The principles of restorative justice work both in school settings and within families. The same challenges apply. Implementing the principles takes time and energy, but the value of what can be instilled in children in learning to correct misbehavior is enormous, especially if done as a method of addressing family problems from an early age. Perhaps the most important item in the restorative justice toolbox is the opportunity to build **empathy** among children from the get-go. When children enter kindergarten without having had the opportunity to think about how their actions affect other people, they enter a social setting with an absolute egocentric viewpoint. Their actions reflect no attachment to others because they have not had the chance to think about their impact on others before making that first misstep in a school setting. Let's see how parents play a critical role in helping their children develop both a sense of empathy and a concept of restorative justice as a means for righting a wrong.

HELPING PARENTS HELP THEIR CHILD
THINK ABOUT RIGHTING A WRONG

Unfortunately, many children today do not come to school ready to learn in a group environment. Their problem-solving skills have been learned from television and video games where problems (translated: people) are beaten, blown up, or shot—and sometimes all three. Children with this mind-set have little empathy for their peers, unless those peers are seen as valuable to the attainment of personal goals. Children with little empathy for others, who are interested only in attaining their own goals, and who have been raised in a video haze of violence are ripe to drift into power-oriented groups. Read that *mobs.* Read that *gangs.* Read that *not healthy for society.*

Parents can be encouraged to begin implementing restorative justice in their homes with nothing more than a few simple questions to their children when they are misbehaving:

- *"How do you think you would feel if your sister had taken your toy away from you?"*

- *"Your behavior today affects more than just you. When you misbehave like that at my friend's house, it makes me sad, especially because I know that you know better than to act that way and I trust you to act better when we visit other people. How do you think my friend felt when you threw that rock at her little boy?"*

- *"Let's think about what you just did. Was that fair to your friend to hide her toy?"*

The object is not to shame, but to make children *think* about their actions in the broader context of the world in which they live. It's important to help children understand that their actions always affect both themselves and others, that we are connected by our behaviors even when we don't think that what we do affects anyone else.

Educators are often puzzled when parents ask them how best to respond to their children at home when the child has committed some infraction at school.

Should a teacher give an opinion about home discipline? Basically, no. School personnel are not in the position to advise parents about how to discipline their children, especially if the question is whether or not physical punishment should be used. Remember, parents look to educators as the experts; therefore, what we say carries much weight with parents who are dealing with their own insecurities about how best to parent a child.

However, school personnel are in a position to offer examples of *alternative forms of discipline* that have a *positive learning component* wrapped into the experience. Parents can be reminded that the best discipline is a correction in which a child learns from the mistake. Let's take the following example as one way to respond to a parent's inquiry about how best to handle the child who has bullied another at school:

Parent [P]:   *I tell you, Mr. Miller, I'm so mad at Simeon right now I could just spank the living daylights out of him! I'm tired of having to come up here all the time and get him when he gets in trouble.*

Teacher [T]:   *Sounds like you're really frustrated with him, Mrs. Damone.*

[P]:   *Frustrated? I want to kill him!*

[T]:   *Well, we certainly don't want that to happen and I'm sure you don't either.*

[P]:   *No, not really. But he just keeps picking on these other kids and it seems like nobody can do anything about it.*

[T]:   *We're frustrated too, Mrs. Damone, both for him and for you.*

[P]:   *I just don't know what to do anymore.*

[T]:   *What have you tried in the past when this has occurred?*

[P]:   *Grounding him from television and his video games. No telephone. Basically trying to make home like a prison for him until he starts acting right.*

[T]:   *And how does he respond to that?*

[P]:   *He hates it, but he knows that he has to do it or we'll just extend his punishment that much longer.*

[T]:   *Have you ever tried to talk with him at home about his behavior here at school?*

[P]:   *Not really. He knows he's not supposed to act like that.*

[T]:   *I'm sure he does. But we're not seeing the correct behavior that we both know he is capable of showing us. Do you think he understands that his actions hurt other people too and not just himself?*

[P]:   *I'm not sure he cares.*

[T]:   *Maybe we can find out.*

[P]:   *How?*

[T]:   *Well, here's what I've been thinking and, if you think it's worth the effort too, maybe this time is a good opportunity to try something different when you and your husband talk to Simeon tonight. I've got three questions I think we need some answers to that will help us understand his behavior better.*

[P]:   *Might as well. Nothing else seems to be working.*

[T]:   *Okay. I think it would be helpful for us to try and get beyond just the punishment part of Simeon's discipline and take it up a notch to helping him take responsibility for his actions. How do you think he would respond if you were to talk to him about making up for the wrong he did to Lacita today in the library?*

[P]:   *What do you mean?*

[T]:   *Today he took three of Lacita's pencils and broke them for, apparently, no reason. While we all are going to penalize him for that behavior—he loses playground privileges with us for two days and he's grounded with you at home—Lacita's still without the three pencils. How do you think he would respond tonight when you talk with him about what he thinks is the right thing to do to make things right again, back to square one, with Lacita? Not that he has to like it or that he has to do it right now, but just try and see if he will agree that the right thing is for Lacita to at least get replacement pencils for the ones that Simeon broke.*

[P]:   *I don't know. We've never thought about that before. We've always focused on the grounding and not on what he needs to do to make up for what he's damaged. That's not a bad idea. But I know he won't agree to it unless we make him do it.*

[T]:   *That may well be the case, but we won't know until you talk to him about it, right?*

[P]:   [Nods head in thought.]

[T]:   *You know, the bigger issue for Simeon, besides correcting his behavior, is in understanding that his actions have hurt Lacita and that he is responsible for righting the wrong, besides just getting caught. If you and Mr. Damone—Vic, right?—can get Simeon to begin the process of understanding that it's not enough to get punished for his bullying, but that a part of being a responsible person is that one also has to pay back the person that he's hurt to help make things right again—that will go a long way toward helping us at school as we try and enforce the same message here.*

[P]:   *That sounds good, but what if he doesn't agree to do it?*

[T]:   *At this stage, we just want to plant the seed of an idea for how he can make amends for his misbehavior. If he agrees to do it, great. If he doesn't, at least for now, it's a start to get him thinking, and that's what we want the young lad to do more of before he acts—think!*

In this scenario, the teacher has provided an opening discussion point between the parent and child to *begin* the conversation about restitution for breaking someone else's property. How the student responds to the parent's probe will provide insight from several angles. First, the intensity of response to entertaining the notion of making restitution is a marker of the depth of resistance on Simeon's part. Is Simeon dead set against the idea of returning pencils to Lacita? How will we know unless we ask? We can always begin to address other aspects of Simeon's behaviors as we move forward—but we have to help parents make that first step.

WHAT HAPPENS AFTER THAT FIRST STEP?

In a perfect world, of course, Mr. and Mrs. Damone would have a delightful conversation with Simeon, and he would gleefully agree not only to return three pencils to Lacita but also to add an entire pack of Empire No. 2s as a gesture of peace to all humankind. However, in this case, I don't think that is likely to occur.

What is important about that first step for parents is just that—taking it! Parents often do not have the energy, and can't come up with the tools off the top of their heads, especially after a busy day working two jobs just to make ends meet, to conjure up the dialogue necessary to talk about a subject about which *their* parents most likely couldn't talk to them. That's where the educator can be of great assistance—by providing talking points and encouragement to them as they begin this collaborative journey with us to help solve the bullying dilemma.

So, what comes after that first step with Simeon and his parents? Let's look at several options in Chart 8.1.

As complicated as this chart might look at first glance, it's really not. The options on the left side all move toward quick resolution of a bullying incident and restitution following a discussion about it with Simeon. The right side of the flowchart involves repeated efforts to keep him engaged in thinking about the incident that will, one hopes, move his decisions back toward the left side of the chart.

What does that right side of the chart discussion between Simeon and his parents sound like? First of all, whomever is talking with a child about misbehavior, be it educator or parent, must do so only when *calm* and *rational* about what is about to occur, especially if the likelihood exists—and it most likely will—that the responses of the child will lean toward the right side of the chart rather than the left. After all, if children were compliant with all our heart-to-heart talks, you probably wouldn't be reading this book anyway.

Chart 8.1   Helping Parents Discuss Bullying and Restitution With Their Children

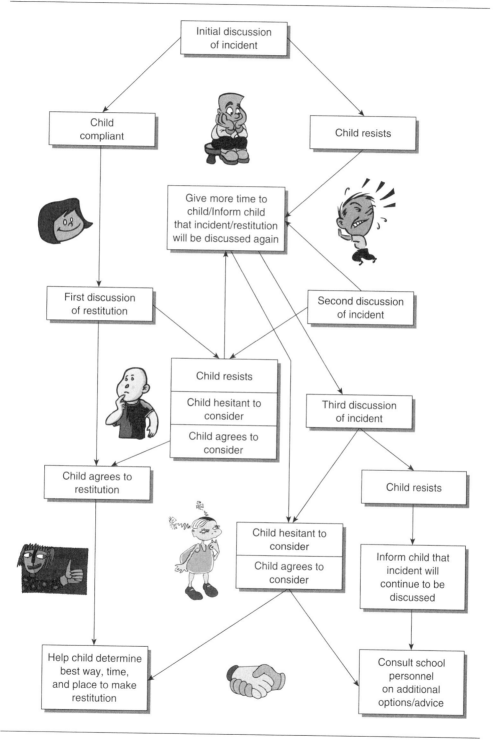

It's important to view the efforts to get children to consider—or reconsider, in the case of the more recalcitrant ones—as a horizontal spiral moving forward. The goal is to keep the child moving in a positive direction. It will likely take several efforts, and some of the topics covered may have to be rehashed. The key to success is to continue to make progress and cover a little more ground in each successive discussion than the time before.

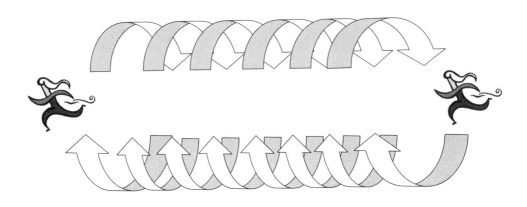

How many times is enough in trying to engage Simeon in seeing the wisdom of moving toward a restorative solution to his actions? The answer depends on the child and the reactions one gets after each attempt to discuss the issue. At some time in a discussion of a difficult topic, especially when each side is trying to convince the other of the wisdom of switching sides, both parties may decide that enough is enough and dig in deeper in defending their positions. At that point, it's probably best that the adults move to requesting additional assistance and consultation from school personnel who are used to dealing with conflict on a regular basis. Some of these personnel include the school counselor and other student services personnel within the school who may have additional avenues of approach with a difficult child.

Experience has taught me that the best techniques to sway opinion on a difficult issue involve *time* and *patience:* time for children to consider the points made in the discussion and weigh the pros and cons of how moving toward what the adult wants them to do affects their status in Kid World, and patience on the part of the adult to wait out the children during the process. How long is an appropriate time to "wait out" the child? Again, it depends on the issue and the child. It is far more meaningful for children to make sincere acts of restitution out of a true desire to right a wrong than for them to make the gesture because they feel as if they are being forced to do so (the always popular, "Yeah, well, I guess I'm sorry because I have to be—but I don't really mean it."). If it takes a child a week, after several discussions, to understand the full meaning of a behavior and be willing to accept responsibility for it, then that is a week well spent. Children and adolescents—particularly adolescents—are adept at holding on to an argument and waiting out adults. *They* know *we* have a tendency to drop discussions of difficult issues and move on because of our own busy lives.

That being said, three tries has a certain logic behind it. First discussions often fail because the initial behavior is still fresh and emotions related to the event may still be high. If a first effort to resolve an issue fails, especially if emotions became a stumbling block, time may loosen the level of intensity of the original event and both parties may be able to move forward toward solution. If two efforts at getting to agreement are not enough, a third try, after additional time, will provide more insight into the degree of ownership that the recalcitrant party is willing to invest in refusing to cooperate. At that point in the process, enlisting those previously mentioned outside resources will bring in different perspectives, but the child needs to understand that the behavior is not going to be forgotten and that it will continue to be discussed until it improves.

In the case of Simeon, the discussion between one of his parents using these techniques may well go like this:

Father [F]:   *Simeon, we need to talk again about what we've been working on the past few days. Would you turn off the television?*

Simeon [S]:   [No response. Keeps watching television.]

[F]:   *Simeon?*

[S]:   [Turns off the television and moves from the floor to a chair next to his father.]

[F]:   *You know, I need your help on this thing. We've talked twice now about what happened between you and Lacita last week, and I'm concerned that you still feel as if you didn't do anything wrong.*

[S]:   *I didn't. She deserved it.*

[F]:   *Not by the way you were raised in this house and by the rules of the school. You know that.*

[S]:   [Says nothing.]

[F]:   *Look, you've already been punished at school and you just got your privileges back here at the house. You don't want to go through all that again, do you?*

[S]:   *No.*

[F]:   *Then your mom and I need some help trying to figure all this out. Do you really believe that what you did to Lacita was right?*

[S]:   [Looks out the window. Says nothing, waiting for his father to move on, but he doesn't. Finally, he answers.] *No, I told you that last time.*

[F]:   *We agree on that. How about what we talked about then too? What would be the best way to make up for what you did with her pencils?*

[S]:   *I don't want to do that.*

[F]:   *Because?*

[S]:   *Because I just don't want to.*

[F]:   *But is not giving her back new pencils for the ones you broke what you would want done for you?*

[S]:   [Says nothing, waiting out his father again.]

[F]:   *Son, we all make mistakes, and a part of learning how to get along with other people is doing what we can to try and make up when we have done wrong to others. You've already said that you know that breaking her pencils was wrong, and I think you also know that the fair thing to do is apologize and give her back some new ones. That's what we would want to happen for you if it was the other way around.*

[S]:   [Still says nothing. Looks at the floor.]

[F]:   [Waits for a few seconds to let his words sink in.]

[S]:   [Still looks at floor, then at his father.] *Well, what am I supposed to do?*

[F]:   *What you know in your heart is right.*

[S]:   [Thinks.] *I don't have any pencils to give her.*

[F]:   *We'll get the pencils for you; that's not a problem. What will you do when you go to school tomorrow with them?*

[S]:   *I don't know what to say.*

[F]:   *We can figure that out tonight. It doesn't have to be much, but it should come from your heart. What would you like someone to say to you?*

[S]:   *Here's your pencils!*

[F]:   [Laughs.] *Well, that's a start.*

Simeon and his father do not have to be perfect in terms of what they work out to say to Lacita. However, every effort should be made to ensure that Simeon is successful so that it increases the likelihood that the next time something goes wrong, he knows that it *is* possible to make amends for misbehavior, especially if it was truly an accident.

The next chapter highlights seven talking points to share with parents to help them talk to their children who are being bullied. Chapter 8 and Chapter 9 together provide you with many helpful hints to share with parents to move them even closer to forming a parent-educator alliance.

CHAPTER NINE

Seven Talking Points for Helping Parents Talk to Children About Being Bullied

The seven suggestions in this chapter offer specific approaches that we can recommend to parents to assist them in talking to their children about being bullied. These seven talking points are for incidents that occur inside a school setting or within the school's jurisdiction. Subsequently, the parent and school personnel must work together since the problem, in these scenarios, occurs under the supervision of the school. Parents can learn to adopt these suggestions for use in other settings, specifically child care or other environments in which adults are in a caregiving capacity and have supervisory authority with children. Figure 9.1 at the end of the chapter lists these talking points in a handout form that might prove helpful to give to parents.

TALKING POINT 1: HELP PARENTS UNDERSTAND THE IMPORTANCE OF LISTENING TO THEIR CHILD'S CONCERNS ABOUT BULLYING AND TEASING

Perhaps the first suggestion is the most important. Listening—*really listening*—to children's concerns regarding what is happening to them sends a strong message that, contrary to typical Kid Logic, parents and teachers actually *do* care what happens in children's lives and *are* willing to try to understand what it is that is bothering them in their relationships with peers.

Listening is not a matter of appearing to listen or appearing to be concerned. It cannot take place with dad behind a newspaper or mom watching TiVo reruns of the day's soaps. Listening involves actually hearing what the child has to say and at levels beyond just what the child expresses in words. In the professional counseling business this is called **empathic listening**, the ability to put oneself in the other person's situation and try to understand how one might feel if faced with the same plight. Empathic listening is not assuming that one truly understands how the other person feels. When parents make that assumption, they often begin the process of not listening because they start to listen to themselves, their own conversations, and their assumptions, rather than to their child. Besides, even if we adults think we have experienced a similar or nearly identical situation and listen from that familiarity (**sympathetic listening**), we still can never truly know with certainty how our children feel because their experiences *now* are different from what ours *were.*

Empathic listening provides the opportunity, if done correctly, to gather a tremendous amount of information about the world of the child who is victimized. These children will tell us about what happens at levels beyond the words, at the levels of the heart and mind at which life experiences leave marks that are not easily, if ever, erased.

Helping parents get to Talking Point 1 might well be facilitated by some of the following prompts:

- *You know, I think that too many times we adults think we're listening to kids when we're really not. So, what do you think about me just sitting here and really, really, really trying to understand what you're saying for a change?*

- *I can't say that I know how you feel, because I'm not you. You're your own person and I know that you see things differently from the way we did when we were kids. But I am trying to learn what it is like to be you, so please keep going and I promise that I will listen even harder than I ever have before.*

- *I had some of those experiences when I was your age. But that was then and this is now, so my way of seeing things may be different from the way you and your friends do today.*

- *You tell me what you want me to hear and then ask me questions about what it is that you just said. If I'm not right, then correct me, okay? I'm really going to try and do my best to listen this time.*

The main point for parents to understand is that they want to *be approachable* with their child when discussing difficult matters. As difficult as dealing with being bullied or teased in school is for children, talking with a parent about it is thought to be even more painful for kids since they often perceive it as an admission that, yes, well, they really *do* need their parents for something after all. This is particularly true as children move into adolescence (Stern & Azar, 1998) and begin that period of **individuation** in which they struggle to become autonomous while at the same time needing food, clothing, and shelter.

Children are more likely to share information than are adolescents because the process of individuation has yet to begin, but neither children nor adolescents will respond to the best of their abilities if they feel as if the person they are talking to is not listening. Children who find it difficult to talk are very susceptible to shutting down during a parent-child discussion or, worse, not even making efforts to engage in the conversation. Those who are victimized may well fall into this category since their quiet demeanor may be a contributing factor to how bullies sense their vulnerabilities. Shy and quiet children, in particular, must be given lots of *encouragement, time,* and *patience* to increase the likelihood that they will share information.

Some sample prompts that may encourage a child to talk and show that a parent is willing to take the time necessary to really listen include the following:

- *Sometimes it's hard to talk about things that upset us, but I'm willing to take whatever time you need to listen.*

- *When you think that you have the words you need to share with me what has been happening, just let me know. I'll make time to listen to you when you want to talk.*

- *You take the time you need to figure out what it is you want to tell me, and then I'll take the time I need to listen when you're ready.*

The main thing that must *not* happen when discussing a difficult issue with a child is to express frustration that the story is not moving along fast enough or to give the impression that the child is not receiving approval for making the effort to tell the story. That is the fastest way to shut down conversation even among adults.

TALKING POINT 2: ASKING THE RIGHT QUESTIONS WILL LIKELY INCREASE PARENT-CHILD COMMUNICATION

First, a caveat about the power of questions. Before we proceed with Talking Point 2, we must understand that when we ask questions we tend to "disrupt" the flow of what was occurring before a question is asked. Once we ask a question, people change the "natural course" of their story line to attempt to answer the question. If distracted or interrupted, they may or may not have the emotional strength or memory to return to the story and share with us additional details that are important for us to know. A basic rule to help parents think about questions they may want to ask during a conversation is this: "Is this question *absolutely necessary* for me to be better able to understand the story line, or will my asking this question now interrupt the train of thought?" Sometimes it is all a matter of timing as to when best to ask a question. Besides, children sharing stories may tell us what we need to know if we let them tell their stories uninterrupted! That will, in the end, make us better listeners in the eyes of those telling their stories.

What kind of questions will be helpful for parents in Talking Point 2? Here are some prompts that parents can use to keep a conversation moving forward:

- *You said you had something important to talk to me about. What's on your mind?*

- *You seemed upset by something today. Is there something I can help you with that will make things better?*

- *That sounds like it makes for a difficult day. My guess is that when those things happen, it makes you feel as if school's not a very friendly place to be. I wonder what we might be able to figure out together that would make the situation better. What do you think we might be able to do?*

- *Are there ways that you have tried to prevent these things from happening? Give me some examples.*

- *Do you think you might have some ideas about what would make this person/these people stop doing what they are doing?*

- *Does anybody else in the school know about what has been happening to you?*

- *Do these things seem to happen to others?*

The important thing to do at this stage is to assure the child that the kinds of questions being asked are not just about details or the who-what-when-where kinds of questions that they are asked so often in their lives. That kind of information is important, but just not yet. The child must know that the initial questions asked by a parent are about his or her well-being, about how the child is doing as a *person*, as someone whose experiences are *valued* and as someone whom *we are concerned about* when there is confusion in the daily travails of life. In doing so, parents send the very loud, yet unspoken message that they can be trusted and that we want to help them beyond the who-what-when-where levels. (It's like the first question we hope we'll have the presence of mind to ask when our children call us to tell us they've just wrecked the new family car: "Are you alright?" We can pull our hair out later about the details of having to deal with the repairs.)

Talking Point 2 is a critical stage for what will come later. It is very important for parents to understand that, if they are to gain more information about the specifics of what has been happening, they must be as **nonjudgmental** as possible during the earliest stages of helping the child open up about the experiences of being bullied. Being nonjudgmental is often hard for a parent to do. It is difficult for a parent to sit idly by and not comment on reports of events in the child's life of which they do not approve, especially if the parent believes that the child has somehow violated family rules or has contributed in some way to the predicament. There will be time for parents to discuss their concerns *later*, but not *now*. Judgment *now* about the child's behavior is not what is needed, with one exception—minimal comments to a child in support of positive behaviors related to the situation will likely encourage the revelation of additional information. Comments in the other direction, however seemingly tame a parent might think they are, will likely be perceived as condemning, and children who are bullied have enough of that in their lives already.

TALKING POINT 3: PARENTS WANT TO OBTAIN AS MANY DETAILS AS POSSIBLE IN AN UNDERSTANDING FASHION

Talking Points 2 and 3 often occur simultaneously, yet Talking Point 3 may need to wait in the sequence of the information-gathering process. Children may find the initial process of explaining their plight very stressful. It is not uncommon for those who are victimized, particularly those who suffer physical harassment, to reexperience many of the same physical and emotional feelings in the retelling of what has happened. This is one of the ugliest aspects of victimization, the potential for children to become so frightened during intimidation that their bodies literally develop heightened psychological and physiological ways of responding to situations that are similar in nature to the intensity of the original event. This phenomenon is referred to as **hypervigilance**, since the child who is affected to this degree is always alert and cued to interpret even the most simple of uncertain interactions with a peer as threatening. In the most severe cases, the potential exists for chronically abused children to develop severe stress reactions that greatly impair their daily functioning. This is not to say or imply that every child who is the victim of an aggressive act is a candidate for traumatic stress, but it is a greater likelihood among those who have a history of receiving chronic abuse, particularly abuse that is both intensely physical and psychological.

Obtaining additional details of what occurs, when, where, with whom, and under what conditions is essential in helping identify the specifics necessary to begin planning an intervention. This is often a tipping point in parent-child interaction and problem solving. The parent is faced with being an interrogator of sorts without trying to look like one—not an easy role to pull off, especially when teens already think that we adults are members of the Spanish Inquisition on our days off!

The following sample questions and observations may be helpful for parents with Talking Point 3:

- *What exactly happened? Help me understand what occurred by starting at the beginning. Please remember all that you can.*

- *When does this type of behavior occur? Is it before school? After school? During school? If it occurs during school, exactly when does it occur?*

- *Where does the behavior occur? In class? Between classes? On the playground? In the cafeteria? On the bus? At the bus stop?*

- *Who creates the problem for you? Is it one person or more than one person? Are there others who watch what happens? If there are others who watch, do they act as if they like what is happening, do they act afraid, or do they just watch and do nothing?*

Make sure that parents remember Talking Point 1's emphasis on *encouragement, patience,* and *time.* Those are important characteristics to practice *all* the time when talking with kids and maybe here even more so. Remember, if a child finds it difficult to share even the least bit of information about an awkward situation, additional questions are likely to be viewed as even harder to answer because of what needs to be covered next.

Victims are often hesitant to share information about the details of their experiences out of a fear of **revictimization**. Revictimization occurs when an individual receives some additional kind of abuse as a direct result of efforts to receive help. It is the number one reason that kids give for not wanting adults to get involved in their plight. Revictimization can occur in one of two ways. First, individuals who ask for assistance with being teased or bullied and are hypervigilant may, as they tell their story, go through the same feelings and fears that they did when they were being bullied or teased the first time. A more common type of revictimization occurs when, after intervention begins, bullies go after those who asked for the assistance in an effort to seek revenge for the victim identifying the agents of their torment.

Having as much detail as possible about the who, what, when, and where of bullying is critical in helping design an intervention plan. For instance, if incidents of teasing are occurring only in one location, such as the gym locker room during dress-out, then relaying this information to supervisory personnel can allow an effective response by increasing general supervision in that area, which will likely decrease the amount of such behavior occurring in the future. Intervention plans to stop bullying do not have to be rocket science. Sometimes what works best for all involved is the plan with the fewest moving parts.

The importance of giving children the *time* and *space* they need to formulate their answers cannot be emphasized enough. Youth are daily bombarded by questions from us adults who, more often than not, grow impatient when we do not get the answer we want or in as timely a fashion as we think we need. My personal favorite is what teachers do in trying to solicit responses from their students: *"Why do you think the* _____ (fill in the blank here of your favorite subject)?" Pause of 2 seconds. *"No one? Okay, here's why. . . ."* I can use this example with a straight face because I used to do this myself in my early days of teaching! Children learn very quickly that all they have to do is not respond and the adults in charge will either (a) give the answer or (b) go on to something else. After a while, every question that an adult asks begins to go into the "blahblahblahblahblah" category.

Children and youth need time to put their thoughts into words. *This is particularly true of young boys* whom we do not always engender with the verbal capacities they truly need to explain their experiences. It is also true of both boys and girls when they are faced with trying to explain an emotional situation, one in which words are, indeed, hard to find to describe what is sometimes so biologically and adrenaline based. Ever tried to describe fear? It is not something that can be described so much as can the behaviors associated with it.

Here is the bottom line to stress to parents: always be patient when the discussion begins. It may be in bits and pieces and take several hours, or even several days. Patience will likely better assist children in telling their stories than the added pressure that comes from parental agitation. Parents do not want to further complicate a child's life in the zeal to help make it better, and peppering them with questions at the wrong moment is a tried and proven way to do just that.

These prompts are least likely to get the kind of information parents want:

- *I wish you would hurry up and tell me what I want to know. We've been wasting time on this for the last 30 minutes, you know.*

- *I'm getting really tired of talking to you about this. I can't help you if you won't even help yourself.*

- *No wonder your teachers think you contribute to the problem. You won't even tell me what's going on.*

These prompts from a parent are far more likely to receive the kinds of answers that are needed:

- *I will take whatever amount of time you need to talk about all of this.*

- *You can come to me when you're ready to share more of your story. I'll wait for you to get the right words.*

- *I don't have anything more important to do than listen to your story and try to work with you in helping to make things better.*

TALKING POINT 4: PARENTS NEED TO ASSURE THEIR CHILDREN THAT THEY WILL WORK WITH THEM TO FIND A SOLUTION TO THE PROBLEM

In discussing with children the details of what has occurred in their lives regarding incidents of bullying or teasing, it is essential to end the initial conversation with words of encouragement that give hope to the child who has been victimized. Here is an example:

- *Well, I can't guarantee that I will be able to stop everything that is happening, but I promise you that I will do what I can to help make things as much better as they can be. Let's put our heads together and see what we think might be the best ways to put an end to this problem.*

Although it is important to provide the child with a promise of assistance, at the same time it is also important not to give false hopes. Parents must be honest about what we parents and educators can and cannot do. None of us has control over others, and we cannot assure that our involvement in the bully-victim solution will result in the eradication of bullying or teasing for a child. But the hope and promise of assistance from a parent are absolutely critical in overturning the typical response that our children are used to receiving: "Just ignore it and it'll go away."

Part of being honest also means being truthful with children about our own feelings. However, as adults, we must temper what we say in the interests of what is best for our child. A parent may *want* to say . . .

- *I can't believe this is happening! How dare that little punk treat you like that! Why, I've got a good notion to go down to that bus stop and give him a whack or two myself and let him see how it feels to be picked on by somebody twice his size!*

Honest feeling? Probably. Best for the child? No. As previously mentioned, we've all seen those parent-invades-the-bus-to-beat-up-the-child's-bully surveillance videos already.

As hard as it may be for them, especially when their child opens up and expresses great emotion about the pain and suffering experienced at the hands of a bully, parents cannot afford to be anything less than the adults they have to be in the midst of such chaos. Adults who respond with anger and with words indicating that revenge is the avenue of response to the insults of intimidation are contributing to the cycle of violence. A better tempered response might well be the following:

- *I'm really sorry this is happening to you and it really makes me feel both angry and sad that it is. You don't deserve to be treated like that. No one does. Let me take a few moments to think and then we'll talk again in a few minutes.*

This line of reasoning provides adults with a "personal time out" when they find it necessary to take a break from the emotional reaction to hearing that their child is being mistreated. It provides them with time to compose a more adultlike response than one shooting straight from the heart of emotion and in words that display the anger that they might first want to express. If angry words are in order, it certainly does not do the victim of aggression any good to hear them. Most likely, they have already heard enough of that in the original victimization and may well have convinced themselves, as is so often the case among those who are victimized, that they are somehow responsible for the maltreatment they have received. Believing that they have upset their parents by telling the truth will only further muddle the issue for children and decrease the likelihood of their sharing additional details because of their fear of further upsetting the adult.

Talking Point 4 provides *assurance* and *support*. Children need to understand that both school personnel and parents are a part of the solution to the problem and that *teamwork* increases the chances that a positive solution will occur. They need to know that a part of the solution to the problem may be sharing information with those in charge of supervision. Parents who help their children understand that preventing bullying is a complicated matter will do much to decrease their anxiety and the assumption that somehow *they* are the cause of the misbehavior of the bully. Support and assurance from parent to child are essential in reducing the uncertainty that children have about talking to parents in general, especially as they move through adolescence and begin to believe that handling problems on their own without help from anyone else is what being an adult is all about. Children and adolescents must learn quite the opposite—that complicated problems may require asking others for help since those other individuals whom we turn to in times of trouble often hold bits and pieces of the puzzle that have yet to be discovered. After all, when we get sick we know we're sick, but we don't know how to heal ourselves—that's why we go to the doctor, who holds that piece of the wellness puzzle.

TALKING POINT 5: PARENTS SHOULD ASK THE CHILD'S OPINIONS AND CONCERNS ABOUT DISCUSSING THE SITUATION WITH SCHOOL PERSONNEL

This is the step when victims may hesitate or show reluctance to move forward. Their primary concern is the fear of revictimization and embarrassment among peers. Their questions are important to all involved in designing an intervention strategy. What will the parent do with this information? What will happen to me when my teachers confront the bully and then the bully comes back after me? How can you ensure that I will be protected if I give you this information, and that nothing further will happen to me? Good questions all.

Children who are victimized need to understand that there are no guarantees about anything in the intervention process except this: *If no effort is made to do something, in all likelihood the abuse will continue.* If an effort *is* made to stop the victimization, it *might* work. It also might *not.* Is this a chance worth taking to try to make things better? The child should be given the option to participate in the decision at every opportunity.

Talking Point 5 is a very important part of the process of helping victims retake control of their lives, or **empowerment**. It cannot be stressed how important the concept of empowerment and reestablishment of control is to those who have had their power taken away. The feeling of powerlessness leads to a sense of **helplessness** and **hopelessness**. In the worst of cases, helplessness and hopelessness lead victims to believe that their lives are not worth living, and we know that victims of bullying have turned such feelings both inwardly and outwardly with deadly consequences (for painful and poignant personal stories from families whose children have committed suicide in the wake of relentless bullying, see http://www.ryanpatrickhalligan.org and http://www.jaredstory.com). A significant part of the healing process is giving back to the individual who is victimized the power to make his or her own decisions. Talking Point 5 may well be the first time in a long time when victims have been given the chance to do just that—make up their own minds about what they want to do about the situation.

Children may well choose, especially at the first opportunity, to not do anything about the situation, so great is their fear of revictimization. Such a decision must be respected. To force an individual to move forward with an intervention before he or she is ready and committed is another form of revictimization. Such is the horrible **double-bind dilemma** in which both victims and interveners find themselves. Unfortunately, such double binds also continue the risk of continued victimization at the hands of aggressors for exactly the same reason—because nothing is done, no intervention occurs, nothing changes in the life of the target. To choose not to choose *is* a choice.

This is where patience, empathy, and compassion must be in great supply for parents and educators. It is also where parents must be able to discuss with victims the pros and cons of doing something versus doing nothing. A suggested approach might include the following:

- *I think I can understand your concerns about what happens if we share this information with the school. If I were you, I'd be afraid too about what could happen if we share this with your teacher and then you just get more of the same kind of treatment at the hands of the bully.*

- *I don't know what will happen if you think we should share this information with the school. But here's what I hope will happen. I hope that if we share this information, that your teachers will be able to help stop what is happening and that the bully will be put on notice that that kind of behavior is not going to be tolerated. Things might work out if we tell. Things also might not. But I truly believe that if you let me talk with the school that we can all begin to work together to help make things better. What I also believe is that if we don't do something, things will only stay the same or get worse.*

- *I want you to decide whether you want me to call the school because it's important to me that you know that you have the power to be a part of the solution to this problem. I believe that you have a great deal more power to help solve this problem than you may think you do. That's why I want you to think about what's best for you, what you want, and what you think is fair to yourself, and let me know later. Take some time to think about everything we've talked about this morning and we'll get together later today to see what you think is best, okay?*

The above suggested language is recommended for situations involving teasing or in instances of mild to moderate cases of bullying. In the same breath, parents should be encouraged to give higher levels of concern to situations in which (1) the teasing or bullying is clearly severe, (2) the child is incapable of understanding what is happening to him or her, or (3) the child is incapable of reasonable and appropriate self-defense. *In any case involving unprovoked violence or violence with injury, recommend to parents that they contact supervisory personnel immediately.* This advice goes against the grain of empowerment, yet clearly severe cases of bullying or teasing require immediate intervention due to the potential for immediate harm. Here is a suggested dialogue for such cases:

- *I really appreciate what you have shared with me. I care deeply about your health and safety everywhere you go. This doesn't sound too safe or healthy for you or other people.*

- *I know that you don't want me to go to the principal about all of this, but the fact is that you're getting hurt at school and that's not good. You don't go there to get beaten up. That's not fair to anybody. My guess is that, based on what we've talked about, the school would do something if they knew what was happening and who was doing it. This is one of those times when we can't keep something private. The kind of treatment you've been receiving is totally unacceptable. I'm not going to let that kind of thing happen to my child.*

- *Tomorrow I'm going to school with you to meet with the principal and see what can be done to stop this. I know you said you don't want me to do this, but this is above and beyond what any child or family should have to put up with. You deserve better than this and tomorrow we're going to start the process of making sure you are safe, sound, and respected.*

Talking Point 5 may be one of the most difficult with which parents will have to struggle. Weighing pleas from children not to intervene on their behalf is a tough call. None of us wants to do anything to make a bad situation worse, and the truth is, as we have stressed in this step, that there is no guarantee that it will not. This is where parents have to make that judgment call as to what they believe is in the best interest of the child. What makes the call harder is the fact that it is not simply a decision that parents can help implement; rather, it is the beginning of a process that challenges a child to dig deep inside and face challenges alone such as when unguarded by adults at the bus stop, on the playground, in hallways, or in bathrooms. It is a tough call, indeed.

All suggestions up to this point have been designed to encourage a conversation with a child who is victimized in an effort to gather information and empower the individual to take the first steps to reclaiming his or her life and self-esteem. Talking Points 6 and 7 are action steps and are designed to take steps outside the home toward solution. These suggestions are relevant as well in assisting parents to work with school personnel in providing a safe environment for everyone.

TALKING POINT 6: ENCOURAGE THE CHILD NOT TO RESPOND TO PROVOCATION WITH VIOLENCE

At some point, children have to return to the environment where teasing and bullying occur. Parents must not send their children out of their homes with the impression that a valid response to the intimidation they receive is a violent one, not even if in their gut that is how they would prefer to solve the problem. Violence only encourages more of the same, and it sets off an inflammatory spiral of additional mayhem that often becomes uncontrollable for everyone involved. Remember, recent incidents have shown that it is more often the bully than the victim who is irrevocably physically harmed when a victim strikes out in rage against the intimidator. Parents and educators must be certain that we do not give explicit or tacit approval for violence as a result of discussions we have in our homes and schools regarding responses to intimidation.

At the same time, children *do* have a right to defend themselves if attacked. I want to strongly emphasize this point: *those who are attacked have the right to defend themselves.* Attacks, in this sense, refer to both **physical** and **verbal** abuse, although certainly one demands a more overt and obvious response than the other. Parents will more than eagerly question us about the traditional educational advice against violence. However, **self-defense** is not just about a physical response to challenges. It also involves the **nonviolent responses** as covered in *Bullying From Both Sides* (see Chapter 8). The tools of self-defense necessary to respond to verbal abuse are much different from those needed to respond to physical assault. Verbal self-defense techniques, which can be learned both at home and in school, are also less likely to result in a victim violating school rules about fighting since, as is so often standard school policy, no distinction is usually made between aggressor or victim in a fight—both typically receive similar, if not the same, punishment (an absolutely brilliant educational practice that truly endears us to the parents of those who are attacked).

Physical self-defense may involve any number of actions, from leaving the scene immediately after receiving a physical blow from an aggressor, to seeking help from an adult, to responding with equal force in an effort to stop and drive away an assailant or protect oneself from further injury. Different situations demand different responses. *Both children and their parents must be fully aware of the consequences involved in using a particular self-defense mechanism and must be ready to abide by the fallout from the use of either one.* Same-kind physical responses to physical attacks will likely be a catalyst for the aggressor to increase the severity of an assault, if not at the time of the target's physical self-defensive action then at another time at the choosing of the aggressor.

Parents and their children must have a thorough understanding of what they think is necessary to respond effectively to intimidation. Learning new techniques takes time, something that neither teacher nor parent has in great supply during periods of uproar such as those found during a bullying episode. If current coping or avoidance mechanisms are not working for a child who is victimized, then new methods and strategies must be learned. These take time to learn, practice, and implement. Likewise, educators will need to be involved in discussing with parents how they can help the child at home practice these newly acquired skills. Results may be slow in coming, particularly when a child must not only learn new effective response techniques but also regain the self-confidence and self-esteem that have been chiseled away by the lengthy effects of bullying.

Children need to know whom they can turn to and where they can go during times of danger to avoid abuse, the main focus of Talking Point 7 below. This is a key to reducing the likelihood that a physical confrontation might occur. When children know they can turn to significant adults or where safe havens are located, they are more likely to use them as additional resources in their nonviolent self-defense repertoire. *Parents must be encouraged to teach their children to let educators know when bullying and teasing occur.*

Here are three possible leads to help parents talk to their children about not responding in kind to rude and bullying behaviors when they occur:

- *I know that what happened today made you very angry and was embarrassing and I also heard you say that you want to do the same back to the ones who did all of that to you. I'm concerned that if you do, it will only make matters worse because it will make those individuals feel as if they are justified in doing it to you again in the future. Let's think about some other ways that we might be able to respond if they try and do that again.*

- *We don't have to hit back every time someone treats us wrongly. Sometimes it's just better to walk away when you think those kids are going to do something to you and move to a safer place. Have you thought of that before? What are the safe places that you might be able to go to when you feel that something bad is about to happen like what happened today?*

- *I know that ignoring their behavior won't make it go away, but until I can meet with your teachers to talk about all of this, it might be best to try and not respond to those individuals who keep picking on you since what they've been doing is just using words. I know that words can hurt, but I also know that sometimes people say things to others so that they can just get a reaction out of them and try and make them mad.*

The bottom line for educators to emphasize to parents is that, if at all possible, they must not encourage their child to respond violently in situations in which they merely feel *uncomfortable*. Parents must help their child understand the difference between feeling uncomfortable and feeling *threatened*. Everyone feels uncomfortable at times, but being uncomfortable should not evoke the same kind of response as being in a threatening situation. Imagine what would happen in social gatherings if people who felt awkward responded violently just because they didn't know many people in the group!

TALKING POINT 7: PARENTS SHOULD ENCOURAGE THEIR CHILD TO ASK THOSE IN A SUPERVISORY CAPACITY FOR ASSISTANCE

Children expect that adults will come to their aid during times of duress. Not only is this a reasonable expectation; it is also an **adult obligation** to respond to a child's requests for assistance. Adults, of course, must not overreact to every request for aid since it teaches children that they can turn to others to solve every problem. Likewise, adults must not automatically turn down every request for assistance from those seeking to escape their tormentors out of the stereotypical belief that "it's kid stuff, they can sort it out themselves."

Children learn early about how adults respond to their concerns. When it comes to bullying and teasing, the typical child and adolescent have developed quite a degree of **cynicism** about how much concern adults have about their plight. Most children will tell you that the reasons they do not tell adults about their concerns related to intimidation are that (1) adults will not do anything about the problem, and (2) if they do tell adults, the resultant do-nothing response of adults only makes the problem worse. Whether or not these beliefs are true becomes secondary to the mythology among children that asking adults for help is a futile effort. *This simply has got to change*, both in fact and in fiction.

Parents should encourage their children to come for help to those adults who serve in supervisory capacities when their children do not have the resources on their own to deal with a difficult situation. In that perfect world we talk about quite often, when children run out of nonviolent resources, adults will know that a request from a child is to be taken seriously, the unspoken message being, "I can't figure this out on my own, anymore. I need your help." In such a scenario, children would know that it is their obligation to first try to resolve a situation, and adults would know that children have tried to do just that before coming to them, and therefore the request is to be taken seriously. *Adults do untold damage to their reputations in the eyes of children when they disregard legitimate requests for assistance.* For the sake of "encouraging" children to "figure things out on their own" and "grow up," faith and trust can be squandered. When children are rejected by significant adults in their lives, they seek answers elsewhere, and we all know that where and from whom our children seek that guidance may, in the long run, not be in a child's best interest.

A proposed conversation between a parent and child about seeking adult assistance might go like this:

- *My guess is that your teacher doesn't know about Josh's poking you in the back of your neck with his pencil in class. I bet she'd like to know. She seems like a caring person and you might be surprised about how she might know just exactly what to do.*

- *You know, if you and your friends are having trouble in the parking lot after school, you might want to talk to a teacher or two that you like and let them know about what's going on. They probably will be more than happy to see to it that the parking lot is supervised more closely, and they might actually catch what's going on when it happens. That seems like one solution to the problem.*

- *I know you said you just absolutely don't want to tell your teachers or any other adult in school about what's been happening in the girls' bathroom during lunch, but if you don't share that information things probably won't get any better and they might even get worse. And if you know the names of the ones who are pick-ing on that new girl, don't you think she might need some help in stopping the harassment? You could be an important part of the solution to another person's problem.*

In the next chapter we discuss the expectations that parents are entitled to have after they have approached school personnel with their concerns about the bullying behaviors their child is experiencing.

Figure 9.1   Seven Talking Points to Help Parents Talk With Their Children About Bullying

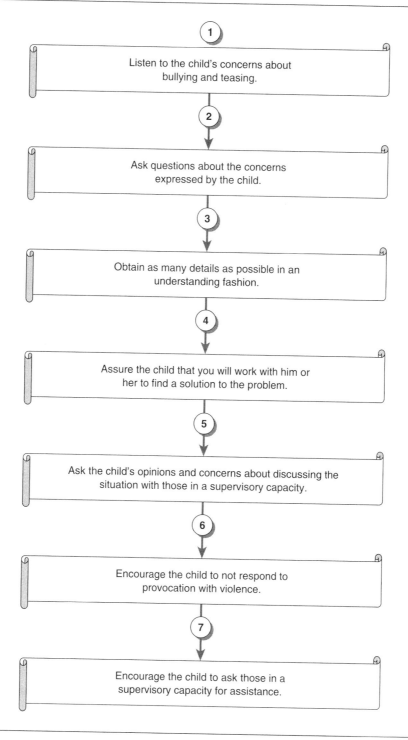

CHAPTER TEN

Fair Expectations of Parents and Educators in Solving the Problem of Bullying

P arents want their children to be safe and sound, especially in the caregiving environments to which they entrust them, be it day care or elementary, middle, or high school. They are profoundly correct to have certain expectations about those caregivers. Parents expect that caregivers are knowledgeable about their profession, that they are appropriately licensed or otherwise duly credentialed to provide their services, and, last but certainly not least (and, perhaps, most important in many ways), that they have the best interests at heart of those whom they serve.

When things go wrong in educational settings, things that children and their caregivers cannot resolve on their own, parents should be appropriately involved in working with supervisory personnel to help improve the situation. But how much is too much involvement? What is the appropriate level of parental involvement in resolving such matters as opposed to simply becoming a "nagging parent" or being viewed as overreacting on behalf of a child?

Here are six fair expectations that educators should meet when responding to parents' concerns about the bullying and teasing of their child. These expectations are best used in conjunction with implementation of the seven talking points discussed in Chapter 8. The six fair expectations are predicated on the assumption that it is a parent's and child's responsibility to *also* make efforts to address a problem *in conjunction with* the supervisory staff. Problems are solved best when they are addressed at the "lowest level" at which they occur—between the parties directly involved. This is commonly referred to as the **geography of problem solving**. The more people involved in the solution to a problem, the more complicated it becomes and, like some Murphy's Law of Machines, the greater the likelihood that someone will not carry through the way he or she was supposed to!

FAIR EXPECTATION 1: NOT ALL BULLYING BEHAVIORS CAN BE STOPPED OR PREVENTED

Some people just run stop signs. Bullies do this all the time until they are given a reason to choose to act otherwise. No matter how hard everyone tries to prevent such behaviors or wishes that they would disappear from the face of the earth, we cannot totally eliminate bullying and teasing behaviors among children and adolescents. It is a phenomenon of the culture, and it is a worldwide problem made even worse by the daily booster shots of vicarious violence via the media that encourage our kids to use violence as a problem-solving tool.

Parents must understand that our children will be exposed to other children (and, unfortunately, even adults!) throughout their lifetimes who have difficult and demanding personalities. Some of these individuals will engage in intimidating behaviors, either verbal or physical. Parents need to inoculate their children early by explaining the simple, but ugly, fact of life that some people we meet in this world are tough to deal with, but that does not mean that there are not appropriate and nonviolent ways to deal with them. We do not realistically prepare our children for the rigors of human interaction if we fail to provide them with this important bit of information, nor do we do them any favors if we instruct them to strike back in kind to whatever intimidation comes their way.

Parents who assume that their children live in a gilded world safe from all of life's injustices will spend many a sleepless night in agony over the very injustices they find their loved ones dealing with on a daily basis. *The anxiety level of parents transfers directly to children.* Kids pick up on the behaviors of those parents who indicate uneasiness about their world or the world of their children. So, while not giving the impression that a report of teasing is to be ignored, it is always better for parents to respond calmly to such reports than to raise the tension levels at home with an overreaction.

Here are some ideas for helping parents understand Fair Expectation 1:

- *At the outset, let me share with you our frustration with the way some children treat their classmates. We don't want anyone to feel mistreated here at school, but the reality is that, while we are dedicated to doing everything humanly possible to try and stop bullying from occurring, it still goes on behind our backs.*

- *We need your help in addressing this problem, but I have to be honest right up front. No matter how hard we try to stop bullying, there always seem to be kids who find another way to do it. While we think we are doing a better job of preventing and stopping it when it happens, we also know that we likely will not be able to catch every instance each time it occurs.*

- *Rest assured, we are going to do everything we can to stop what has been happening from happening again. But I have to tell you the truth—some kids are really hard to work with and I cannot guarantee you that they won't figure out a new way to keep pestering their peers at the very moment we let our guard down.*

FAIR EXPECTATION 2: ONCE BULLYING HAS BEEN REPORTED, THE PARENT HAS THE RIGHT TO EXPECT THE SUPERVISORY AUTHORITY TO INDICATE CONCERN

Healthy supervisory leaders want healthy environments for those in their care. Healthy learning environments create an atmosphere of safety and increase the chances that positive learning will occur. Supervisors know that when negative experiences occur in their place of business, everyone suffers in some way. The suffering might be direct, as in the case of the child who is bullied, or indirect, as in the tarnishing of the reputation of an entire staff or organization that is perceived by the parent as allowing bullying behaviors to occur.

Who do parents assume is capable of "doing something" to stop the bullying of their child? It depends on the setting. It could be the *director of a day care center* or a *teacher* in charge of the classroom setting in which such behaviors happen. It might be the *bus driver* or the *playground monitor.* Certainly, it would be the *principal* of a school and, following the chain of command upward, ultimately the *superintendent* of schools and perhaps even the *governing board.* All parents know is that those in charge are supposed to be able to protect their child from harm, and they are certainly entitled to have that expectation.

But parents must also understand that there is a specific protocol that needs to be followed so as not to alienate the supervisory authority at the first call. It does no good to call the president of a company about a late delivery of a package when the problem lies with the delivery service. Systems have a mechanism with which to respond to complaints, and those who do not follow the prescribed methodology are destined to become ensnarled in it. So, parents who need to express a concern over an incident of bullying behaviors must be helped to "play by the rules" of the organization they are challenging. There may well come a time when going higher up the chain of command is necessary, and I am the first one to advocate doing so—when the time comes—*but it is not prudent for a parent to launch a full-scale assault on an entire organization when the problem may well be best addressed at the lowest level at which it is encountered.* Remember that geography of problem solving? Parents will gain from being helped to understand how the school system works and how it solves the problems that they bring to the system's attention.

Parents need help in determining to whom their concern should be reported. It is just as important to get a concern routed to the person who is most likely to be effective as it is to voice the concern in the first place. There are most likely policies in public educational settings that require specific procedures to be followed when a concern about harassment arises. There may well be specific individuals who are in charge of starting the information-gathering process in order to both protect the individual and develop an effective intervention plan. In smaller settings such as day care centers and private schools, or in rural settings, it may be customary for all such calls to be handled by the owner or principal. Size makes a mighty difference in both how much supervision children receive and how long it takes for an effective intervention plan to be enforced.

Educators too must avoid panic when a complaint or concern about bullying that occurred on their watch comes forward. A *nonthreatening inquiry* from a parent does not cast any aspersions on the school or school personnel and increases the likelihood that we will not react defensively to what is simply a matter of sharing what should be to all a mutual concern about the health and safety of kids. Having a mutual concern also increases the *sense of a cooperative venture* for all parties and the likelihood of attaining that win-win solution for everyone. Negative and accusatory tones from educators tend to alienate parents and decrease their enthusiasm in wanting to help.

The effective supervisory authority will be concerned about the matter and will start some kind of intervention as soon as possible. "Starting some kind of intervention" does not mean solving the problem at the first attempt. (Well, if it does, then that's great, but don't count on that happening on a regular basis.) Sometimes, assigning adult supervision to a previously unwatched area will reduce or eliminate the problem. At other times, bullying is a complicated problem requiring a multifaceted approach. But all caring and concerned supervisory personnel will start as soon as humanly possible to do something to alleviate the problem behaviors.

Possible responses to such notification of a problem might include the following:

- *Thank you for letting us know about this matter. We will get started on it first thing tomorrow morning to see what we might be able to do.*

- *I'm really sorry to hear that this has been occurring. I will personally meet with John tomorrow to learn more about this and notify the bus driver too as to what has been going on.*

- *We have a Peacemakers team here that addresses just such problems. If you and John do not mind, I would like to have some of those team members meet with John tomorrow and see if they can't give him some ideas on how to avoid those problems while we also figure out a way to stop the behavior from occurring in the first place.*

As long as the lines of communication are open, everyone feels as if they can talk more honestly with one another. That honesty and openness will come in handy should the problem become more difficult to solve. *One of the best ways to stifle further cooperation between parents and educators is through the failure to give the respect due to those concerns the first time they are expressed.* It is important to remember that, by the time most parents act on behalf of their children, a problem is likely to have existed for quite some time. This is especially true in dealing with the revelation between parent and child that bullying has been occurring. Kid World rules are explicit, particularly during adolescence: Turn to adults only if the problem is really, really a big one! So, by the time word gets back to educators through parents about a problem occurring with their child, the clock has most likely been running for a long, long time.

FAIR EXPECTATION 3: PARENTS EXPECT THE SUPERVISORY AUTHORITY TO INVESTIGATE THE CONCERN

Effective and healthy organizations do not object to receiving information about a problem within the system. *Healthy organizations want to know where problems exist so that they can begin the process of seeing what can be done to eliminate or correct them.* One marker, then, of an effective school in which bullying has been reported is the willingness of staff to begin the process of discovering everything that it can about the situation in order to start the improvement process.

But what is meant exactly by the term *investigate*? Are we talking about calling in the FBI or the CIA to interrogate little Susie's classmates as to what they know about the incident with little Johnny at 2:18 P.M. on June 15, 2006? Not exactly.

Effective educators listen to what was reported by the concerned parent or party and take notes to help with further actions that might prove helpful or needed. The most effective supervisors will have some kind of mechanism in place to begin the process of follow-up with such information. Schools will most likely have a policy in place that designates the process that is to be followed when reports of harassment emerge. *The best educators know exactly how to proceed and do not flinch or become defensive when a matter of bullying and teasing comes to their attention.*

Unfortunately, because so often parents report the peer abuse of their children with great vigor and with a tremendous amount of emotion, the people on the receiving end of the phone or visit are often forced to go immediately into a defensive posture since it appears that they are being personally attacked. Parents might need to be reminded that, no matter how much it may appear that the person at the other end of the phone is nonchalant or lackadaisical about the matter, the chances are pretty good that *that* individual is not responsible for the peer abuse that has been occurring. Although adults may have culpability in how and why peer abuse continues, they are not the ones who are in the third grade themselves and have been tripping that parent's daughter on the way to the lunchroom every day. (If they are, better call the police and social services quickly!) And as mentioned in Fair Expectation 2, putting a potential problem-solving party on the defensive at the very outset is not the best way to inspire a desire to get started or dig more deeply into a matter of mutual concern.

An effective supervisor will determine how best to proceed within the particular environment once an initial parent report is received. Those adults closest to the "scene of the crime" should have an understanding of the dynamics of how such behaviors are occurring. They may also have insight as to behaviors on the part of the victim that the child may not have reported to the parent. Children do not always tell the complete story. (Well, parents know that *other* people's children do not always tell the complete story—*theirs* do, of course!) Effective educators, however, will take the information from a source, assume it was provided with the best of intentions, and treat it as factually as possible without passing immediate judgment. Most stories, like a coin, have more than two sides. Think about that one and you will see that it's true.

The effective educator will make a determination of the best method by which to begin. It is important to get as much information as possible from as many different angles as available—don't forget that three-sided coin. Of course, a major contaminating factor in beginning a fact-finding mission is the request that may have been made by the child to the parent to "not do anything" or to "please don't tell" the very educators who must be consulted. Parents must understand that once they refer such a matter to a supervisory authority, it begins a domino effect that all parties involved may not be able to control completely. Parents need to be helped in understanding that in the chaos of untangling the Gordian knot of bullying, things have a tendency to sometimes get worse before they get better.

Gather as much information as possible from all relevant parties. Such information gathering might include verifying the information in the referral from the parent; consulting with others in a supervisory capacity as to whether they have observed similar or corroborating behaviors on the part of either the alleged aggressor or the victim; directly observing the area in which such behaviors are supposed to be occurring; and conducting direct but separate interviews of both the alleged aggressor and the victim.

After conducting such a fact-finding exercise, the supervisor can make a better decision as to how best to take the next step and what kinds of immediate action may be necessary. Such gathering of information might be a matter of being in the right place at the right time the very next day, or it might take days to fully conclude that, yes, indeed, there is a problem that needs to be addressed. Patience may be in order for parents.

Several sample responses to parental expressions of concern include the following:

- *Ms. Graves, I will be better able to help solve this problem if we can agree to talk to each other in a more calm fashion. I appreciate your concern about your son because I'm concerned too about what you're telling me happened. But I can't be as helpful if I feel as if you're attacking me for something that another child did to Charles.*

- *Again, Ms. Nyberg, thank you for sharing your concerns with us about Nancy. The incident you reported is helping us discover some weak areas in our playground supervision that we didn't know existed. We're continuing to see what we can find out about everything that happened last week, and we will keep in touch with you as we go along.*

- *No, Mr. Beasley, I'm not ignoring your concerns. I've just been listening and making notes about what you're telling me so that we can follow up on this matter as soon as possible and help Joe.*

- *Ms. Edwards, you have to understand that as much as I would love to tell you that all of this will be solved immediately, I can't give you that guarantee. This problem is one that involves several students, and as we try and sort it all out, it will take time. But you have my word that we will do everything we can to correct the problem as soon as possible, and we will be in touch with you as we move forward.*

As shown in these sample dialogues, keeping in touch with parents is a key factor in increasing the chances of keeping the doors of communication open.

FAIR EXPECTATION 4: APPROPRIATE INTERVENTION WILL TAKE PLACE IF THE CONCERNS ARE VALIDATED

This particular expectation will have to occur when it has to occur. It may or may not come before Fair Expectation 5.

Educators have an obligation to provide for the health and safety of those individuals for whom they are caring. Sometimes immediate action is necessary. If an incident of peer abuse is confirmed and occurs daily in the setting in which supervisors are available and have the authority to intervene, especially if such bullying presents the potential for harm to the abused, then not only is immediate intervention warranted, but failure to intervene may well be an act of negligence.

Appropriate intervention may involve a series of steps. The most immediate intervention is a notice to the perpetrators of the following:

1. They may not do such acts in the future.

2. Such behaviors are not tolerated in the setting.

3. If they persist in such behaviors, they will be held accountable.

4. They owe the victim of their abuse an appropriate apology within the framework of working to make things whole again.

A message that a bully will be removed (suspended or expulsed) from the setting should be reserved for the most extreme of cases. The focus of an intervention at this stage should be on immediate correction of the misbehavior and safeguarding the victim from additional abuse. Follow-up is needed, of course, for both intimidator and target to enhance the chances that something positive will be salvaged from such a negative interaction.

Parents have good reason to assume that actions will be taken to address the reported incident of peer abuse. However, it is not always possible for supervisors to respond in a fashion that parents may want or in as quick a fashion as desired. Smaller organizations (in-home day care, small schools, or private schools) are likely to have fewer obstructions and less red tape to ensnarl a supervisor than in larger settings, such as in public schools, where the same rules in place to protect children often create the burden of paperwork or procedures that slow the process— *any* process—dramatically. One big pitfall, which is both good and bad, is how supervisory personnel dance around the issue of confidentiality and privacy. By the same token, a smaller institution's personnel, without such a protocol, may make decisions without a full understanding of their ramifications ("Why did you do it that way?" "Because I could, that's why."). Sometimes it is best to proceed with caution and with rules that provide guidance and a road map in the midst of stormy weather.

FAIR EXPECTATION 5: THE SUPERVISORY AUTHORITY WILL COMMUNICATE WITH PARENTS AS TO THE OUTCOME OF THE INTERVENTION

Parents want to know what happens to their children, especially when they are under duress. Effective supervisors will share as much information as is possible with parents. They may not, however, be able to share all information about incidents because of the privacy or confidentiality rights afforded to children and families. (This was mandated by law in public schools under the Family Educational Rights and Privacy Act of 1974 [Public Law 93-380] and later modified by sections accompanying the USA PATRIOT Act of 2001 [Public Law 107-56] and the No Child Left Behind Act of 2001 [Public Law 107-110].) Private institutions may or may not have the same requirements to protect student and family privacy, but it is a common courtesy at the very least to shield personal information as much as is possible when discussing conflicts between children with parents.

Parents expect to hear from supervisors in a "timely fashion," but timely by parental definitions and timely by a supervisor's definition may be in two different time zones. A parent's focus is solely on the child. The educator's focus is on hundreds of kids, many with needs just as great and challenging as the one with which the parent has requested assistance. This is particularly true in large public schools where parents with requests may have to "get in line" before a supervisor can begin to respond. Often the urgency of a response is determined by priority level, beginning with those in the most danger, in the most trouble, or with behavioral deficits creating the largest uproar for the total school setting.

Being reasonable is an important characteristic for parents to develop in dealing with callbacks from teachers. Patience is the key. Parents, however, will not "roll over" and agree with something that they do not understand or assume that an intervention was successful if they did not hear back from educators about what has been done in response to their concerns. It is not enough to be told that an immediate intervention was successful. Questions need to be answered about how such incidents will be prevented in the future.

An effective response from a supervisor in a day care setting might well go like this:

I wanted to get back in touch with you about your call yesterday on the incident between Jamie and Andy.

I watched the two of them very closely today during snack breaks and playtime and you were right about Andy getting a little too pushy with Jamie. Today he seemed to want to snatch Jamie's snacks and had a great interest in the same toys that Jamie picked up. I spoke with Andy about what I had seen him doing and he was quick to say that he was sorry to me and that he would not do it again. He seemed to be genuine in his behavior and even apologized to Jamie and gave him a hug after I spoke with him. By the end of the day they were playing together well and were sharing toys.

The staff will keep an eye on the two of them to make sure that that behavior doesn't happen again, and we will also keep a lookout to make sure that no other children have similar problems. If you have any concerns again, please do not hesitate to let us know.

An effective response at the middle-school level might well go like this:

Thanks for your call the other day about the incidents that had been happening between Joel and Hakeem. We did not know that they had been having a conflict and we were glad to be able to get to the bottom of the problem. But it isn't as clear-cut a matter as we all thought that it was at first.

First of all, because Hakeem did not want us to talk to Joel about the matter, it slowed us down in our response. We let Hakeem talk to Mr. Hogan, the school counselor, about the best ways that we all might be able to work on the matter, and finally Hakeem and Mr. Hogan worked out a plan which Hakeem felt better about and so we went with it.

Because Mr. Hogan had met with Hakeem and had his side of the story, we had him also meet with Joel to see what he had to say. Joel at first denied having anything to do with any bullying behaviors, but then later agreed that he had done some of the things that you reported to us. He also provided some additional information that indicated that Hakeem had also played a part in what originally started and Hakeem agreed, afterMr. Hogan talked with him again, that he had, indeed, done some things to Joel but that he had only done them in self-defense.

So, here's where we are now. Both Joel and Hakeem are meeting with Mr. Hogan individually to begin working on the rules we have here for instances just like this. It's called the Fair Play Plan, and you can find it in your parent's handbook for the district, which was sent home with each student at the beginning of the year. With that plan, Joel will work with Mr. Hogan to review his behavior in school with his peers and see if it needs improvement with anyone else besides Hakeem. Mr. Hogan will also meet with Hakeem to make sure that he is okay and to discuss any other issues which Hakeem might want to share as a result of this incident. Later, both Joel and Hakeem will meet face-to-face in Mr. Hogan's office so that Hakeem can tell Joel what he needs to about how this matter has affected him and so that Joel can apologize to Hakeem and the two of them can begin to work on a plan to make sure that behaviors like this don't happen again. Joel will also receive an in-school discipline because of what he has been doing to Hakeem, but that is separate from his work with Mr. Hogan. Hakeem will not be disciplined, but I will have to warn him that he can't always expect that hitting back in self-defense will be tolerated at school and that if it occurs again, he will need to get assistance from the nearest teacher on duty as soon as he can. Mr. Hogan and the boys will also be working on a plan so that Joel knows that there are other ways that he can handle his anger and so that Hakeem knows that there are other ways to avoid being picked on without hitting back.

We are really glad that you brought this matter to our attention because we did not know that that area of the building was a problem area and we can now put staff out there to make sure that it is better supervised. So, we are very grateful that you brought this matter to our attention so that we can make our school a better place for everyone who goes here.

If you have any questions, please do not hesitate to contact me in the future.

Notice that in both of these scenarios, the amount of information that was shared was tempered so as to protect the privacy of the children as much as possible. Additionally, the supervisors were not defensive. They were clear on what they had done to respond to the initial report and on what their responses were. They left the door open for additional interactions on the part of the parents. Such *nondefensive responses* help everyone feel as if there are solutions to the problem at hand.

FAIR EXPECTATION 6: NEVER FORGET FAIR EXPECTATION 1—NOT ALL BULLYING BEHAVIORS CAN BE STOPPED OR PREVENTED

As much as parents would like our professional efforts on behalf of their children to yield results, they have to come to grips with the reality that there are some things that, unless either they place their children in a plastic bubble or we follow them around 24 hours of the day, will not be able to be changed. One of those nasty little realities of life is that bullies have that uncanny ability to strike when least expected and in spite of all our best intervention techniques, efforts, and intentions. It is important for parents to remember that supervisory personnel of children have many responsibilities for which they are accountable. Although a parent's focus will undoubtedly be on the single beloved child in the family who is in need of assistance, supervisory personnel cannot provide the same kind of singular guarantee for children.

However, when efforts by supervisory personnel to stop bullying and teasing seem to be ineffective, a parent may well go into the What's Wrong With Those People Don't They Care About My Child They Never Do Anything for Anybody parent mode. Anger at the perceived failure of others to whom parents entrust their children to provide adequate protection is natural. Mother Bear and Father Grizzly parental responses do serve a purpose now and then to "encourage" a foot-dragger to speed things up, but for the most part, educators end up viewing those kinds of responses as overreactive and overprotective. Who wants to work with someone who—literally or figuratively—has just poked a finger in our eye and then expects us to work with them to solve whatever problem it was that got them so upset.

Parents have a right to have certain questions answered about the reemergence or continuation of negative behaviors directed toward their child. Was the latest incident a singular occurrence or another in a series of events? Bullies often randomly pick on others just to seek out the most vulnerable. Was the incident directed not only at their child but at others as well? Sometimes teasing and bullying are directed toward several children in a group. A child who has been subjected to such behaviors in the past may be overly sensitive to the reemergence of these behaviors directed at others and may assume that the taunts were directed more at him or her. Was the aggressor the same one who was previously involved in the intimidation of their child or was it someone new, and if it was someone new, was there a connection between the original harassment and this new event? Sometimes intimidators will get their cronies to do their bidding for them if they know that they are being watched or if the penalties are too high for their own involvement.

The answers to these questions are critical before a new intervention strategy can be designed. If the most recent incident was truly an isolated occurrence, then it may have been just that—a random effort to rattle someone's cage. If there is a connection to previous bullying or a pattern to the latest incident, then apparently the original intervention was ineffective. And whether we like it or not, we need to know if what we, as educators and supervisors, are doing is not working.

A subsequent request by parents after an original intervention plan should be met with different expectations, especially if the reoccurrence of bullying was not a one-time incident and, most certainly, if it continues. Ultimately, parents have the right to pursue all avenues at their disposal to protect their children. Sometimes this involves removing a child from an environment that is not safe. It may involve legal intervention to force the aggressors to stay away from their child. Restraining orders are not out of the question, though they are often difficult to enforce. Holding supervisory personnel accountable if they neglect their duties in affording reasonable protection for the children under their care is another option, be that entity in a public or private setting. Sadly, I have consulted with many parents who have exercised all of these options. Personnel in charge of children are *not* responsible for negative behaviors among peer groups that they cannot predict or stop. They *are* responsible and accountable for attempting to effectively intervene in such behaviors when they know of their existence. In one instance, a mother who was a school board member in a North Carolina school district very publicly resigned her board position in protest of school personnel's inability to stop the incessant bullying affecting her son ("Local Woman," 2004). In a Washington State parochial school, parents sued on behalf of their 14-year-old boy who was not protected from students who, as the lawsuit alleged, "engaged in a concerted campaign of assaults and outrageous conduct perpetrated against the plaintiff" (Turnbull, 2004); in Connecticut, another family sued a public school on behalf of their 10-year-old son who was "bullied . . . [shoved] into the wall . . . sucker punched and tripped" ("Hamden Parents Sue," 2004). Each of the parental alternatives noted above were last-ditch efforts by desperate parents and caused a tremendous amount of emotional upheaval, not to mention the possibility of great inconvenience, for all concerned—children, parents, and educators. Children do not want to leave their peer groups. They do not want to be seen by their peers as running away from a problem. Depending on the age of the child and the seriousness of the intimidations, legal intervention such as restraining orders or pressing charges may be perceived by children as mortifyingly embarrassing.

The bottom line, however, never changes: In the end, educators must do what they believe is in the best interests of the children. Parents also need help in understanding what their actions may mean to the world in which their children live. Parents have little patience when they feel that their children are threatened, but it is sometimes the most valuable commodity they can provide for them as they learn to maneuver through the intricate spiderweb of life.

CHAPTER ELEVEN

The Courage to Act

One of the founding figures of modern-day counseling, Alfred Adler, believed that the most difficult challenge facing us in daily living was mustering the courage to act on our convictions (Mosak & Maniacci, 2008). How true. It takes courage to do what we know we must to combat intimidation within our schools. A key element of this challenge is our willingness to venture into a realm previously ignored in educational circles by inviting parents to join us in the partnership to prevent the bullying and teasing of our children in school.

This effort may not be as difficult as we fear. More often than not, when we offer parents assistance we find that they are more open to receiving it than we had imagined. One of the drawbacks of the culture within our schools is that educators have so much to do that the task of any additional conferencing with parents about "one more thing" takes on a straw-that-broke-the-camel's-back proportion. "I just don't have the time to do it" is a common lament within schools, and it is very, very true. The reality is that if educators were not willing to take their work home with them and sacrifice personal time to grade papers, read and prepare reports, and write letters of recommendation, half of what is accomplished in schools wouldn't happen.

But conferencing with parents about student progress and difficult issues can occur *only* during the school day. More specifically, holding parent-educator conferences about behavioral matters is a *primary obligation* of school personnel, as is dealing with the behavior of those who bully their peers or those who are victimized by such behaviors. As we have noted, for far too long educators and parents have chosen to ignore this problem, as if receiving abuse from peers is a normal developmental stage that is a prerequisite for moving from adolescence into adulthood.

Courage sometimes includes admitting to past mistakes. For those who are reading this book and have found themselves evaluating some of their past responses to bullying as tepid at best, the courage to act begins the next moment they set foot in the school building with a new resolve to respond more effectively to the problem. It makes no difference what rationale the individual has used in the past to justify ignoring the problem—that was then; this is now. I have met many educational professionals during my years of leading workshops across the country who have come to me afterward and admitted that they had not done as effective a job responding to school intimidation as perhaps they now recognize they should have. My response is always the same: "Recognition of an error is the first step to knowing what needs to be done better. We all make mistakes. It takes courage to change course."

I hope that these supportive statements have encouraged (Hmmmmm. Look what root word is embedded there!) teachers, counselors, social workers, and administrators to act differently than they have in the past, and that they will be words that all of these groups can use with parents during their parent-educator conferences on this topic. Parents need support in working with their children just as much as educators do. The Greek philosopher Philo is often credited with saying, "Be kind, for everyone you meet is fighting a hard battle." Such words of wisdom are well remembered by parent and educator alike. It is essential to remember that both parents and educators have "hard battles" to fight. For some, those battles are small aggravations (paperwork, being late for an event because the car wouldn't start, spilling milk). For others, they are incredibly draining (prolonged illness, poverty, domestic violence). Both educators and parents bring these small and large battles with them into parent-educator conferences. Is it any wonder that sometimes things don't go as planned for either party?

For those who have been actively involved in fighting the good fight to prevent and intervene in school bullying, first and foremost, you deserve a hearty thank you from all the parents and kids in your school (and me, too, if that makes any difference). Your willingness to go that extra mile—to do not only what you "have" to do by virtue of rules and regulations but also what is the *morally right* thing in helping reduce school violence and make children's educational experiences the best they can be for all concerned—is exactly the kind of exemplary behavior we want and need from *all* educators. Our actions *always* make a difference. Whether we choose or fail to act, there are always consequences that follow. They may not be evident in the immediate aftermath of an event, but time will out the full measure of the choices we make. Those who choose to ignore intimidation send a message that bystanders have no role in the fate of others. Children learn that individuals are on their own, that when they are attacked by bullies, no one will come to their aid. When we accept the challenge of responding to adolescent peer-on-peer abuse, we send the message that such behaviors are not acceptable and will not be allowed in the school setting. When we add parents to the mix as a part of the solution process, children learn that the caregiving circle is much larger than only the school or home. It is large enough to include both and, with that, the role models who live within.

Courage for educators also comes in the form of motivating colleagues and parents previously on the fence to get involved and take the first steps to do more. It is leading by example through the implementation of the ideas that are generated from this book and others. Take the ideas and concepts generated within these chapters and make them your own. Take the sample scripts and give them your own voice. *You* are the expert. All you need is the courage to act!

References

American Academy of Pediatrics. (n.d.). *Understanding the impact of media on children and teens.* Retrieved November 22, 2006, from http://www.aap.org

Amstutz, L. (2000, Spring). Where to from here? *Conciliation Quarterly, 19,* 11.

Anderson, C., Gendler, G., Riestenberg, N., Anfang, C., Ellison, M., & Yates, B. (1998). *Restorative measures: Respecting everyone's ability to resolve problems.* St. Paul: Minnesota Department of Education (formerly Minnesota Department of Children, Families & Learning).

Associated Press. (2006, February 6). "Credible threat" closes Warroad schools. WCCO TV [Minneapolis, Minnesota]. Retrieved December 9, 2006, from http://wcco.com

Augsburger, D. (1992). *Conflict mediation across cultures: Pathways and patterns.* Louisville, KY: Westminster/John Knox.

Bandura, A., Ross, D., & Ross, S. (1961). Transmission of aggression through imitation of aggressive models. *Journal of Abnormal and Social Psychology, 63,* 575–582.

Bowers, L., Smith, P., & Binney, V. (1992). Cohesion and power in the families of children involved in bully/victim problems at school. *Journal of Family Therapy, 14,* 371–387.

Bowers, L., Smith, P., & Binney, V. (1994). Perceived family relationships of bullies, victims and bully/victims in middle childhood. *Journal of Social and Personal Relationships, 11,* 215–232.

Carney, A., & Merrell, K. (2001). Bullying in schools. *School Psychology International, 22,* 364–382.

Centerwall, B. (1992). Television and violence: The scale of the problem and where to go from here. *Journal of the American Medical Association (JAMA), 267,* 3059–3063.

Corsini, J., & Wedding, D. (2008). *Current psychotherapies* (8th ed.). Belmont, CA: Thomson Brooks/Cole.

Craig, W., Henderson, K., & Murphy, J. (2000). Prospective teacher's attitudes toward bullying and victimization. *School Psychology International, 21,* 5–21.

Cronkleton, R. (2005, August 12). Taunted teen wins federal suit. *Kansas City* [Missouri] *Star.* Retrieved August 13, 2005, from http://www.kansascity.com

Dana, D. (2001). *Conflict resolution.* New York: McGraw Hill.

Dawson, D. (2006, July 31). Girls take school to court, saying it ignored bullying. *ABC News* [US]. Retrieved December 2, 2006, from http://abcnews.go.com

DeVoe, J., & Kaffenberger, S. (2005). *Student reports of bullying: Results from the 2001 school crime supplement to the national crime victimization survey* (NCES 2005-310). Report of the U.S. Department of Education, National Center for Education Statistics. Washington, DC: U.S. Government Printing Office.

Drew, N. (2002). *Six steps for resolving conflicts.* Retrieved November 26, 2006, from http://www.learningpeace.com

Eron, L., Huesmann, L., & Zelli, A. (1991). The role of parental variables in the learning of aggression. In D. Pepler & K. Rubin (Eds.), *The development and treatment of childhood aggression* (pp. 169–188). Hillsdale, NJ: Erlbaum.

Family Educational Rights and Privacy Act of 1974 (FERPA), Pub. L. No. 93-380, (20 USC § 1232g; 34 CFR Part 99).

Fisher, R., Ury, W., & Patton, B. (1991). *Getting to yes: Negotiating agreement without giving in* (2nd ed.). New York: Penguin.

Fultz, V. (2006, February 9). Schools locked down after scare: Officials issue code red alert for entire school system. *Suwanee* [Suwanee County, Florida] *Democrat.* Retrieved December 9, 2006, from http://www.suwanneedemocrat.com

Gerzon, M. (2006). *Leading through conflict: How successful leaders transform differences into opportunities.* Boston: Harvard Business School Press.

Hamden parents sue school over bullying. (2004, April 24). WTNH.com [New Haven, Connecticut]. Retrieved April 26, 2004, from http://www.wtnh.com

Hurst, M. (2004, November 17). Researchers target impact of television violence: Helping children divide TV fantasy from reality becomes a top priority. *Education Week, 24,* 8.

Imrite, R. (2006, September 17). Accused teen's mom says he was bullied at school. *Press Gazette* [Green Bay, Wisconsin]. Retrieved December 11, 2006, from http://www.greenbaypressgazette.com

Integrated Curriculum for Achieving Necessary Skills (ICANS). (n.d.). *Steps to resolving conflict with others.* Retrieved November 26, 2006, from http://www.literacynet.org

Johnson, K. (2006, April 23). Students had hit list, mayor says. *USA Today.* Retrieved April 24, 2006, from http://www.usatoday.com

Kabel, M. (2006, April 21). School death plot revealed. *Kansas City* [Missouri] *Star.* Retrieved April 24, 2006, from http://www.kansascity.com

Kaiser Family Foundation. (2003, October 28). *New study finds children age zero to six spend as much time with TV, computers, and video games as playing outside.* Kaiser Family Foundation Press Release. Retrieved November 22, 2006, from http://www.kff.org

Kaiser Family Foundation. (2005, September). *The effects of electronic media on children ages zero to six: A history of research.* Retrieved November 22, 2006, from http://www.kff.org

Kressel, K. (2006). Mediation revisited. In M. Deutsch, P. Coleman, & E. Marcus (Eds.), *Handbook of conflict resolution* (2nd ed., pp. 726–756). San Francisco: Jossey-Bass.

Limber, S., & Snyder, M. (2006). What works—and doesn't work—in bullying prevention and intervention. *State Education Standard, 7,* 24–28.

Local woman wants bullying issue to hit general assembly: Former school board member seeks better definition, enforcement of bullying. (2004, April 22). WRAL-TV [Raleigh, North Carolina]. Retrieved May 10, 2004, from http://www.wral.com

McEwan, E. K. (2005). *How to deal with parents who are angry, troubled, afraid, or just plain crazy* (2nd ed.). Thousand Oaks, CA: Corwin Press.

Media Awareness Network. (n.d.). *Research on the effects of media violence.* Retrieved November 11, 2006, from http://www.media-awareness.ca

Mediation Works. (n.d.). *7 steps to resolving conflict.* Retrieved from http://www.mediation-works.org

Meryhew, R., Burcum, J., & Schmickle, S. (2003, September 26). Cold Spring school shooting: Horror hit in seconds. [Minneapolis, Minnesota] *Star Tribune.* Retrieved December 2, 2006, from http://www.startribune.com

Meryhew, R., Haga, C., Padilla, H., & Oakes, L. (2005, March 21). Rampage at Red Lake High School: 10 dead, 12 wounded. [Minneapolis, Minnesota] *Star Tribune.* Retrieved December 2, 2006, from http://www.startribune.com

Moore, C. (2003). *The mediation process: Practical strategies for resolving conflict* (3rd ed.). San Francisco: Jossey-Bass.

Morley, M. (2006, November 28). *Violent video games leave teenagers emotionally aroused.* Radiological Society of North America. Retrieved November 29, 2006, from http://www2.rsna.org

Morris, W., & Morris, M. (1988). *The Morris dictionary of word and phrase origins.* New York: HarperCollins. (Original work published in 1977)

Mosak, H., & Maniacci, M. (2008). Adlerian psychotherapy. In R. Corsini & D. Wedding (Eds.), *Current psychotherapies* (8th ed., pp. 63–106). Belmont, CA: Thomson Brooks/Cole.

Nansel, T., Overpeck, M., Pilla, R., Ruan, W., Simons-Morton, B., & Scheidt, P. (2001). Bullying behaviors among US youth: Prevalence and association with psychological adjustment. *Journal of the American Medical Association (JAMA), 285,* 2094–2100.

National School Boards Association. (2005, September). *Greenwich Public Schools settles bullying lawsuit.* Retrieved December 2, 2006, from http://www.nsba.org

Newman, K., Fox, C., Harding, D., Mehta, J., & Roth, W. (2004). *Rampage: The social roots of school shootings.* New York: Basic Books.

Newsome, B. (2005, November 19). Students suspended over website. *Gazette* [Colorado Springs, Colorado]. Retrieved November 19, 2005, from http://www.gazette.com

No Child Left Behind Act of 2001, Pub. L. No. 107-110, 115 Stat. 1425 (2002).

Office of Human Resource Development, Office of Human Resources, University of Wisconsin–Madison. (n.d.). *8 steps for conflict resolution.* Retrieved November 26, 2006, from http://www.ohrd.wisc.edu

Ohio Literacy Resource Center. (n.d.). *Working with difficult people.* Retrieved November 26, 2006, from http://literacy.kent.edu

Olweus, D. (1993). *Bullying at school.* Malden, MA: Blackwell.

Perlmutter, T. (1994). Parenting in the television age. *Child & Family Canada.* Retrieved November 22, 2006, from http://www.cfc-efc.ca

Phrase Finder Discussion Forum. (2000, October 5). *Re: Sticks and stones.* Retrieved February 12, 2006, from http://www.phrases.org.uk

Pippin, M. (2006, November 17). Middle school bullies and their victims. *Joplin* [Missouri] *Daily.* Retrieved December 9, 2006, from http://joplindaily.com

Ragsdale, J. (2006, January 31). 39 knew of Red Lake killer's plan: Family members say federal officials told them that Weise had discussed school shootings since 2003. *St. Paul Pioneer Press.* Retrieved December 2, 2006, from http://calbears.findarticles.com

Reinberg, S. (2006, November 28). Video game violence goes straight to kids' heads. *Washington Post.* Retrieved November 29, 2006, from http://www.washingtonpost.com

Rigby, K. (1993). School children's perceptions of their families and parents as a function of peer relations. *Journal of Genetic Psychology, 154,* 501–513.

Rigby, K. (1994). Psychosocial functioning in families of Australian adolescent school-children involved in bully/victim problems. *Journal of Family Therapy, 16,* 173–187.

Rispoli, M. (2006, November 14). Court ponders bullying bias. [Cherry Hill, New Jersey] *Courier Post.* Retrieved November 19, 2006, from http://www.courierpostonline.com

Roberts, W. B., Jr. (2006). *Bullying from both sides.* Thousand Oaks, CA: Corwin Press.

Rose, L., & Gallup, A. (2006). *The 38th annual Phi Delta Kappa/Gallup Poll of the public's attitudes toward public schools.* Retrieved September 30, 2006, from http://www.pdkmembers.org

Sander, L. (2006, September 30). Wisconsin principal is shot, killed in struggle with teen. [Minneapolis, Minnesota] *Star Tribune,* p. A4.

Schultz, M. (2004, October 25). Parents use courts to battle bullies: Families take legal action to protect children as schools step up preventive programs. *Detroit* [Michigan] *News.* Retrieved April 2, 2005, from http://www.detnews.com

Schwartz, D., Dodge, K., Pettit, G., & Bates, J. (1997). The early socialization of aggressive victims of bullying. *Child Development, 68,* 665–675.

Seaberg, M., & Sclafani, T. (2006, February 3). Meet Jaba the nut: Driver hit for "Star Wars" fight club on school bus. *New York Daily News.* Retrieved December 9, 2006, from http://nydailynews.com

Smith, P., & Myron-Wilson, R. (1998). Parenting and school bullying. *Clinical Child Psychology and Psychiatry, 3,* 405–417.

Stern, S., & Azar, S. (1998). Integrating cognitive strategies into behavioral treatment for abusive parents and families with aggressive adolescents. *Clinical Child Psychology and Psychiatry, 3,* 387–403.

Titelman, G. Y. (1996). *Random House dictionary of popular proverbs and sayings.* New York: Random House.

Turnbull, L. (2004). Kent family files lawsuit over bullying at school. *Seattle* [Washington] *Times.* Retrieved May 9, 2004, from http://seattletimes.nwsource.com

USA PATRIOT Act of 2001, Pub. L. No. 107-56, 115 Stat. 272 (2001).

U.S. Department of Education, National Center for Education Statistics. (2005). *The condition of education 2005* (NCES 2005-094). Washington, DC: U.S. Government Printing Office. Retrieved November 22, 2006, from http://nces.ed.gov

U.S. Department of Education, National Center for Education Statistics. (2006). *The condition of education 2006* (NCES 2006-071). Washington, DC: U.S. Government Printing Office.

U.S. Office of the Surgeon General. (2001). *Youth violence: A report of the Surgeon General.* Retrieved November 11, 2006, from http://www.surgeongeneral.gov

Williams, T. M. (1986). *The impact of television: A natural experiment with three communities.* New York: Academic Press.

Index